Culture in Crisis and the
Renewal of Civil Life

Culture in Crisis and the Renewal of Civil Life

Edited by
T. WILLIAM BOXX
and
GARY M. QUINLIVAN

To Brent

J. William Boxx
Gary Quin

ROWMAN & LITTLEFIELD PUBLISHERS, INC.
Lanham • Boulder • New York • London

ROWMAN & LITTLEFIELD PUBLISHERS, INC.

Published in the United States of America
by Rowman & Littlefield Publishers, Inc.
4720 Boston Way, Lanham, Maryland 20706

3 Henrietta Street
London WC2E 8LU, England

British Cataloging in Publication Information Available

Library of Congress Cataloging-in-Publication Data

Culture in crisis and the renewal of civil life / edited by T. William
Boxx and Gary M. Quinlivan.
p.   cm.
Includes bibliographical references and index.
1. Civil society. 2. Culture. 3. Values. I. Boxx, T. William, 1953–
II. Quinlivan, Gary M., 1952– .
JC336.C85   1996   306—dc20   96–18235   CIP

ISBN 0–8476–8287–0 (cloth : alk. paper)
ISBN 0–8476–8288–9 (pbk. : alk. paper)

Printed in the United States of America

⊖™ The paper used in this publication meets the minimum requirements of American
National Standard for Information Sciences—Permanence of Paper for Printed Library
Materials, ANSI Z39.48–1984.

In Memoriam

Alex G. McKenna

Exemplum ad Imitandum

Contents

Preface

What does it mean to say that we live in a time of cultural crisis? "Crisis" is from a Greek word meaning "decision." The connotation is that of being at a point where crucial decisions must be made. The deep and widening social pathologies of our time and a disassembled public consensus bear witness to a culture in a state of crisis, compelling decisions at the most profound and public levels. Culture is the social web of customs, rituals, and beliefs, standards of right behavior and wrong, and aesthetic expressions. It is the collective spirit that inspires our sense of beauty, goodness, honor, and duty and our understanding of human nature and creation. It is the moral and intellectual core of what constitutes civilization. In sum, culture includes all that which gives transcendent meaning and order to personal and social life. Quite starkly, we are faced with a choice of destinies. Either to publicly reembrace the notion that life in society is necessarily based upon the presumption of enduring truths and a transcendent moral order or by default to inexorably slide into the barbarism of nihilism.

It is especially the idea of moral consensus derived from traditional under-standings or at least consensus that carries any status in the public square that postmodern ideology has denied. In essence, postmodernity is self-idolatry. We are as gods subject to nothing higher than ourselves and able to remake ourselves into whatever images we may imagine, without any ultimate constraints or con-sequences. The question of values is one of only individualistic inclinations. It is moral relativism writ large in the heavens and often ideologically propounded as if it were from Heaven. This postmodern ideological turn evokes its own negative consensus, a consensus that renders suspect the "tried and true" as a new understanding of the human person is put forth. It is an understanding of human nature as radically free; therefore, any social constraint upon the individual will and personal predilection can be considered as nothing other than a censorious assault. Each person is self-creating and determines his or her own values, such that there are no overarching values, no transcendent principles guiding conscience and behavior that can be confidently acknowledged as both private and public norms.

There is a bizarre contradictory logic at work in this distorted vision in that it demands public atheism and moral relativism as an absolutist value for the political, legal, and educational institutions of society. At worst, this vision is a totalitarian impulse in service to its own overarching value system of relativism. More benignly, it is a misguided civil libertarianism disconnected from community and tradition. True culture is not possible under such a scenario because as Richard Weaver said, "cultural life depends upon the remembrance of acknowledged values." The effectively socialized individual calls to mind what has been taught and what continues to be affirmed in society. That which has been handed down as true and held by all people of good character must necessarily resonate in his or her conscience, deviations notwithstanding, and the institutions of public life must reinforce the formation and dictates of conscience.

It is precisely this internalization of socially acknowledged values that is at stake in the cultural crisis. For culture requires the transmission of such knowledge from generation to generation, conducted through families, supportive social structures, and accommodating civic authorities. The excesses endemic to postmodern ideology, manifested in popular culture and public policy alike, follow from denying the legitimacy of publicly affirmed social norms for moral and civic socialization, thus severing personal conduct and commitments from social order and impeding significantly the transmission of cultural knowledge. Postmodernity denies the validity of such a public consensus because it denies that there are any transcendent principles of moral order governing human nature and sociopolitical life.

The application of relativism to civic institutions effectively removes the foundations of republican government. The principles from which the American political order are derived cannot stand when the idea of enduring verities is swept away. It is contradictory to speak of "these truths" and "unalienable rights" deriving from the "Creator" and of the legitimacy of government stemming from "the laws of Nature and of Nature's God" when the very notion of truth or transcendent principles is considered fictitious. Government cannot then be thought of as instituted to "secure these rights," but rather government itself becomes the author of all rights. Relativism removes any limit on the powers of government with ominous portents for freedom, and democracy becomes merely a process of never-ending competing petitions, which become increasingly difficult to adjudicate or restrain. In the long run, freedom is not possible absent a transcendent order. Neither can civic traditions or the lessons of history be confidently held up as exemplary and unifying when the very notion of common heritage is considered prejudicial or even oppressive. When such an establishment of ideological "diversity" so overwhelms unitive ties, the idea of a common civic heritage inevitably disappears leaving only *pluribus* without *unum*. One can only ask in vain what it means to be a good citizen when the fundamentals of civic life have become so ambiguous and civic heritage so dissipated. Pluralism is only meaningful within a framework of unity, or else it is mere separatism breeding antagonism and finally dissolution.

Acknowledgments

The cultural crisis is largely a crisis of the moral core of civil society and, therefore, affects the major institutions and very structures of civilization. The work of cultural renewal is necessarily eclectic. Thus, this book is interdisciplinary in approach with essays treating various aspects of culture and public life by scholars and experts in the fields of economics, government, philosophy, politics, public policy, social criticism, and theology. All but three of the essays were adapted from papers presented in a conference called "Culture in Crisis" held on the campus of Saint Vincent College in Latrobe, Pennsylvania, on April 5, 1995. The conference was sponsored by the college's Center for Economic and Policy Education. The essay by T. William Boxx titled "Christian Principles and Public Life" was written independently for publication. Robert Royal's essay "The Restoration of Citizenship and Civic Culture" was previously published by the same editors and center in *Public Policy and the Restoration of a Civil Society*. It was adapted from a lecture delivered on September 14, 1994, at a conference called "A Clergy-Business Dialogue on Economics and Policy," also sponsored by the center and held at Saint Vincent College. Finally, Gertrude Himmelfarb's essay "The Renewal of Civil Society" was based on a lecture she presented at Saint Vincent College on October 24, 1995. Her lecture was the sixth lecture in the Center for Economic and Policy Education's Government and Political Education Series.

The editors wish to express their gratitude to Saint Vincent College for providing the academic environment that made this book possible. Saint Vincent College, whose motto is *veri justique scientia vindex*, "learning is the best advocate of truth and justice," is celebrating its sesquicentennial during the 1995/96 academic year, and we are proud to have this book be part of that celebration.

Strong appreciation is expressed to Rt. Rev. Douglas R. Nowicki, O.S.B., the archabbot of Saint Vincent Archabbey, chancellor of Saint Vincent College and Saint Vincent Seminary, and to Rev. John F. Murtha, O.S.B., president of Saint Vincent College from March of 1985 to June of 1995, who have both strongly supported and encouraged the efforts of the Center for Economic and Policy Education. Thanks to James L. Murdy, chairperson of the Saint Vincent College

Board of Directors and chief financial officer of Allegheny Ludlum, who introduced James Q. Wilson's lecture. Gary Quinlivan wishes to thank Br. Norman W. Hipps, O.S.B, provost, and Brent D. Cejda, Ph.D., academic dean, for the release time granted him to work on the conference and this book. William Boxx wishes to gratefully acknowledge the influence of his former teachers at Saint Vincent Seminary, especially those who first taught him New Testament scholarship, Br. Elliott C. Maloney, O.S.B., Ph.D., and Fr. Demetrius R. Dumm, O.S.B., S.T.D.; and also the theology faculty of Duquesne University, especially his Christianity and society teacher James P. Hanigan, Ph.D., his hermeneutics teacher William M. Thompson, Ph.D., and his New Testament teacher Michael Cahill, Ph.D. Boxx also wishes to thank Robert Royal, Ph.D., for his helpful comments.

    A special thanks to Joseph F. Reilly, director of Saint Vincent Theater and instructor of film, and Rev. Martin R. Bartel, O.S.B, the current president of Saint Vincent College, for moderating the sessions of the center's "Culture in Crisis" conference. Appreciation is also expressed to Christine M. Bender, the Center for Economic and Policy Education's program coordinator, and to Don Orlando, the Saint Vincent College publicity director, for the immense amount of assistance they provided in making the conference a success. We wish to thank the following students for their valuable assistance to the center and to the conference: Scott E. Avolio, C'96; Carla L. Burkhart, C'95; Thomas M. Cherpko, C'96; Marcus H. Chlystek, C'95; Brett M. Dias, C'97; Jason E. Farabaugh, C'97; Adam D. Gasper, C'96; David M. Hansz, C'96; Matthew A. Halloran, C'97; Kenneth R. Hemminger, C'98; Aaron B. Hinde, C'97; Amy L. Jeroski, C'95; Kevin P. Kane, C'96; Jaime M. Kochis, C'97; Michael P. Lambert, C'96; Sean A. Lombardi, C'95; Gregory E. Loya, C'95; Ann Marie Lund, C'98; Sean E. McClain, C'96; Kristen L. Sagath, C'95; Amy M. Sikora, C'95; John F. Straub, C'95; Liana M. Swalligan, C'95; Heather M. Threlfall, C'95; Gregory S. Thome, C'97; and Thomas S. Wesolowski, C'95. We would also like to thank Rev. Robert A. Sirico, C.S.P., Dr. Max L. Stackhouse, and George Weigel for reviewing our book and providing several kind comments.

    Finally we are in debt to the following foundations whose support made the "Culture in Crisis" conference and this book possible: Aequus Institute, Earhart Foundation, the J. M. Foundation, the Krieble Foundation, Massey Charitable Trust, Philip M. McKenna Foundation, the Saint Gerard Foundation, Alex C. Walker Educational and Charitable Foundation, and one anonymous foundation.

1

Culture, Crime, and Human Nature

James Q. Wilson

The cultural war is very much the same as the one that you discuss around the family dinner table and in private conversations with your friends. It is about this question: What is wrong with America? Most Americans, when they are interviewed, say that they are reasonably satisfied with their own lives and reasonably optimistic about the prospects for themselves and their families. But that same majority says that they are dissatisfied with the condition of America and not at all optimistic about its future.

What is this condition? I think it is this: People, whether the scholars who have written chapters in this book or ordinary folk in their daily conversations, feel surrounded by a culture that is hedonistic and self-indulgent—is indifferent to the future, heedless of consequences, and failing in personal responsibility. They may exaggerate this problem but it is a widely shared judgment. I would like to tell you how, in my opinion, we got to our present condition. I will use crime as an example. Crime has risen sharply not only here but around the world. Bear in mind that crime is a proxy for an array of problems; to the extent the failure of our culture has contributed to the crime problem, it has contributed, in like measure, to other problems as well: public disorder, graffiti, out-of-wedlock births, and drug abuse.

To understand how we got here, we must understand the second half of the eighteenth century. The Enlightenment was that remarkable period in the history of the West, duplicated in no other part of the globe, when man acquired the belief that he could understand himself by the use of unaided reason. He wished to do this in order to throw off superstition, useless custom, the rule of despotic monarchies, and the preaching of revealed religion. You may understand why people wanted to emancipate themselves from kings and some customs but not why they wanted to free themselves from revealed religion. It was because in the preceding two centuries, Europe had been the scene of brutal religious wars and religious persecution. Intellectuals began to associate religion, or at least the leaders and institutions of organized religion, with intolerance and persecution. Those responsible for the Enlightenment—David Hume, Adam Smith, Adam Ferguson, Immanuel Kant, and others—did not wish to repudiate religion and in some deep sense were believers in the Almighty. But they thought that if man's own reason could provide a sufficient guide to his conduct in this world, then we might achieve the same kind of moral and political progress that the application of scientific reason had achieved in the material aspects of this world. They defended free inquiry and natural reason. The most enduring legacy of this teaching, at least for modern philosophy, turned out to be a single paragraph in one of the books written by David Hume. When he wrote his *Treatise of Human Nature,* he included a passage in which he said that in his conversations with other people he had never encountered an account of what he called a "vulgar" system of philosophy without noticing that in that account the speaker would move imperceptibly from statements about what *is* to statements about what *ought* to be, and would make that transition from an "is" statement to an "ought" statement without justification. Hume argued that morality rested not on reason but on sentiments. For this view and many others, he was thought impious and denied a professorship in any of the universities of Scotland. He did not mean, I think, what many people today think he meant. He did not mean by the separation between reason and sentiments that reason was the only true way of knowing and that sentiments were an inferior way of knowing. He only meant that they are different ways of knowing, each with its appropriate role in human nature.

By the 1920s in the Vienna Circle and in various Continental and British universities, positivistic philosophy became the basis of virtually all modern ethical theory. Though Hume had only said that reason and sentiments are different and that morality rests mostly on the latter, his principle was taken to mean that moral statements, because they could not be verified by the techniques of empirical science, were, strictly speaking, meaningless.

Now that I have given you the beginning and the end of the story, let me reveal a little bit about what happened in between. The Enlightenment gave birth to the West. What we are, we are in large measure because of that period. Indeed, it is interesting that we think of ourselves as part of "the West," which is to say we define ourselves in terms of our geographical location, not in terms of any shared doctrine or ideology. We do not define ourselves in terms of a shared ideology or doctrine because in some fundamental sense we don't have one. What we have is a common ancestry, an ancestry traced back to many thinkers in the second half of the eighteenth century on the Continent and on the British Isles. The view that man is capable by the free exercise of reason and the free expression of preferences—in politics, philosophy, and economics—of understanding and improving his own condition did in fact emancipate man from poverty and despotism. The gains we received in science, technology, and material abundance still astonish the world.

There were, however, problems associated with these developments. I already remarked that David Hume was thought to be impious. Some people began to worry whether this preoccupation with science would undermine morality. That concern haunted Charles Darwin, animated many of his critics, and led him to avoid ever writing about religion because he feared what the implications of his scientific theory might mean for the religion he had absorbed from his own family and friends. Other people worried that the rise of democracy by revolutionary means would undermine tradition. For Edmund Burke this worry was at the heart of his bitter, brilliant, and trenchant attack on the excesses of the French Revolution. Still others worried that the pre-occupation with individual rights might lead to self-indulgence. That last worry centered on writings of John Stuart Mill, a man whose life spanned most of the nineteenth century and who when he died was the philosopher laureate of England.

Mill wrote many books, but he is best remembered for an essay called *On Liberty*. In that essay he set forth a prescription for the right relationship between man and society. It was a radically individualistic prescription. Let me quote from the opening passages from *On Liberty* published in 1859.

"The object of this essay," he wrote, "is to assert one very simple principle as entitled to govern absolutely the dealings of society with the individual in the way of compulsion and control, whether the means used be physical force, in the form of legal penalties, or the moral coercion of public opinion." He was objecting to two kinds of coercion, that of the law and that of convention. "The principle is," to continue the quotation, "that the sole end for which mankind are warranted, individually or collectively, in interfering with the liberty of action of any of their number is self-protection."[1] Or to put it simply, my right to swing my arm ends where your nose begins, but if my swinging my arm does not threaten your nose, then no matter how I swing it or what else I do, I cannot be condemned either by law or by opinion.

That principle led Mill to endorse the decriminalizing of public drunkenness, prostitution, and opium possession. Sound familiar? These policies were not invented by Milton Friedman or Robert Nozik; they were invented by John Stuart Mill 140 years ago. But what is forgotten is that there was another side to Mill. This was the Mill who was in every inch of his being the complete Victorian gentleman. He feared scandal, he disliked public indecency, and in some of his other writings he said things which, if interpreted literally, suggest that he didn't trust people freely to use the unfettered liberty that he had defended in his famous essay.

Let me quote from an essay he wrote about the same time called *The Spirit of the Ages,* which gives you a side of Mill that is not often remarked on. "If you once persuade," he wrote, "an ignorant or a half-instructed person, that he ought to assert his liberty of thought, discard all authority, and . . . trust solely to his own judgment, and receive or reject opinions according to his own views of the evidence, . . . the merest trifle will suffice to unsettle and perplex their minds."[2] Even in *On Liberty* he had remarked that true liberty had to be denied to "children and barbarians."

As Gertrude Himmelfarb has shown, there were two rival John Stuart Mills, two rival aspects to nineteenth-century England, and so two competing aspects of the cultural legacy that we have inherited from that period. One is the legacy of free reason; the other, the legacy of settled convention. By the end of the Victorian period, the natural restlessness that intellectuals bring to any form of constraint or convention had begun to assert itself. In England, in the United States, and on the Continent, intellectuals, artists, and philosophers began to rebel against the legacy of convention, against what we now think of as the stuffiness of Victorian life.

All of you have heard these stories about Victorian culture. The legs of a table were to be referred to as limbs, and if possible covered with petticoats. A pregnant woman should not be referred to as being pregnant, but as in an "interesting condition." Most of what we remember in this vein either is false or was ridiculed by Victorians themselves. After all, Victorian England was filled with writers who regularly criticized the stuffiness of Victorian life. Charles Dickens comes to mind, as does Anthony Trollope. But by the end of the Victorian period, intellectuals had begun not simply to mock its excesses but to deny its premises. The attack constituted what we now call Modernism.

Modernism meant, and still means, many different things, but it meant at that time the belief that human emotions, but especially the emotions of the gifted and the talented, were the best guides to art and convention. We associate this view, for example, with the writers connected with the Bloomsbury set, such as Virginia Woolf and Lytton Strachey. We remember the Armory show in 1913 in New York City in which for the first time Dada art was displayed to a shocked American public. You may recall seeing photographs of Marcel Duchamp's famous painting *Nude Descending a Staircase,* which looks like a series of blurs on the canvas. You only knew it was a nude descending a staircase because he told you so. This assertion of individuality, of private visions, of a rejection of conventional opinion meant that the legacy bequeathed to us by Mill, the twin legacies of radical individualism in principle and constrained communitarianism in practice, was being broken asunder with only the radical individualism left. The constraints had to go.

Intellectuals in England, the United States, and Europe have always criticized their own cultures. Socrates criticized Athens; Machiavelli criticized Florence; Rousseau criticized France; some people, including myself, criticize the United States. Why should the views of a group of intellectuals ever make a big difference in the lives of ordinary people?

Perhaps they might not have made any difference at all had not certain events occurred. Let me mention three. The first, and perhaps the most important, was the First World War. When it began, two-thirds of the Oxford undergraduates volunteered for service in His Majesty's government and went off to fight the Kaiser. By the end of that war, after years of mindless carnage to control but a few yards of a desolate battlefield, a new generation of young men at Oxford swore an oath never again to fight for king or country. The Great War seemed to bring home to the average person the futility of science and reason and the emptiness and hypocrisy of the code of conduct of the Victorian era.

Science had given us what? Poison gas. Technology had given us what? Machine guns and barbed wire. And as far as duty, honor, and country, why, those were simply slogans that had dragged millions of young men off to an ignominious death in the trenches of northern France. World War I profoundly affected all of the West, but particularly England, France, and Germany, and after a time the United States as well. It seemed to discredit everything that remained of the Victorian period. It seemed to leave this message: Do your own thing; there is nothing else to live for. If your country summons you, be suspicious.

Lytton Strachey, the author of *Eminent Victorians*, perfectly captured the spirit in which this war was seen by certain intellectuals.[3] He was asked whether he intended to fight in the war to save civilization. To which he supposedly responded, "I am the civilization they are fighting to save." This attitude of detachment and self-indulgence became the ethos of the 1920s. It was in the 1920s, not the 1960s, that the fundamental changes in Western culture occurred. Freud became the rage. He was widely received in the United States even though he detested the United States and everything it stood for. Religion was rejected, not simply religious institutions but religion generally; religiosity was ridiculed in the public accounts of the Scopes trial and in Sinclair Lewis's novel about an evangelist, Elmer Gantry. Morality was suspect. Self-restraint was described as oppressive, self-expression as desirable. Rights became trumps. Society, not individuals, came to be regarded as the cause of human problems.

The advent of Marxism and Fascism reinforced these tendencies. Marxism added the dangerous notion that human beings are perfectible; with the right social arrangements, created by a violent revolution and managed by a cadre of elite leaders, people can be reconstituted and society rebuilt. The idea commended itself enormously to people convinced that there was no such thing as a fixed human nature. Since society was the cause of all of mankind's ills, a reengineered society could be the cure of those ills. Fascism, or the reaction to it, added a new dimension. Fascism asserted the doctrine of racial superiority. There had long been racists in the United States and in Europe. In reaction to racism and Fascism, scholars, particularly anthropologists and sociologists, began to argue that no culture is superior to another culture, all cultures are equally worthy, and one culture cannot judge another culture because the standards by which you can judge a culture are entirely interior to that culture. There are no transcultural, universal standards that would entitle somebody in one culture to judge another.

These views—Marxism as something to aspire to, Fascism as something to rebel against—and the shattering experience of the Great War helped spread the adversary culture of the intellectuals beyond their salons. The intelligentsia broadly defined—not simply the producers of art, literature, and music, but all people interested in the world of ideas and symbols, whether as producers or as consumers—began to stand in opposition to their own society because it was bourgeois, Philistine, and corrupt. This view was evident in Sinclair Lewis's novels about Main Street, George Babbitt, and Elmer Gantry, and in Sherwood Anderson's account of Winesburg, Ohio. Small-town America was now viewed as the source of everything that was wrong with bourgeois society.

When we took time out for the Depression and the Second World War, these ideas were put on hold for a while. If I am correct, the 1960s can be seen as a resumption of a cultural struggle that began in 1890, came to fruition after the First World War, made great headway during the 1920s, and then was put on ice for a few decades while other business was attended to. By the end of the 1960s, views which already had their antecedents at the turn of the century began to receive full expression. Among these views were the following: Marriage is not a commitment, it is a contract open to renegotiation, and hence divorce ought to be possible on the basis of no-fault laws. Drug abuse increases self-awareness; hence one ought to encourage experimentation with drugs because heightened self-awareness is the highest form of self-realization. Mental illness is a fiction because the keepers are more insane than the kept, and therefore the asylums should be closed. Education should be nonjudgmental because no teacher has the right to impose his or her values on other students. Children have the same rights as adults, and so schools should not be able to expel troublemakers without an elaborate due process hearing. Single-parent households are alternative lifestyles, equally legitimate as two-parent families, and so it is wrong to stigmatize illegitimacy.

It is highly doubtful that, with but a few exceptions, these ideas were accepted by ordinary people. To ordinary people, these views went against the grain. Perhaps the only one that ordinary people might have been prepared to endorse was the liberalization of divorce laws. For the most part, these were the ideas of a self-conscious intelligentsia. There is not a drug that has entered common use in this country, with the exception of marijuana, that did not have its virtues first proclaimed by the intelligentsia. Ordinary people didn't think mental illness was a fiction. They knew about crazy Uncle Charlie; they didn't know quite what to do about him, but they didn't think he was a social construction. Ordinary people didn't think education should be nonjudgmental; with their endorsement, public education in this and every other country has combined technical with moral instruction since the day the schools were first founded. The idea that children have the same rights as adults would be greeted with hoots of derision in any family arguing about who is going to do the dishes. And as far as single-parent families being appropriate alternative lifestyles, this was not a view proclaimed by the heads of single-parent families.

Now, the views of this expanded intelligentsia had an impact on some people. They didn't have much of an impact on most people, but they did have an impact on those people who were particularly vulnerable. The vulnerable people today, as in the 1960s or the 1920s, are those who are young and experimenting with the exciting independence and threats of adolescence; they are people living in neighborhoods abandoned by the middle class and trying to make sense of a threatening and disorganized environment; they are people who are impulsive thrill seekers; and they are people who think of themselves as members of marginalized or oppressed groups. All of these persons are at risk from any set of new ideas in ways that the intelligentsia are never at risk. If affluent people act on these ideas, they will have more troublesome children than what otherwise might be the case. Their children will wreck homes during an occasional wild party, smash up their fancy cars during occasional wild rides, and spend some time in a drug rehabilitation program after a wild bender. But there are therapists, counselors, and clinics with which to manage these difficulties. There will of course be divorce, but there will be remarriage and there will be some kind of financial settlement.

But the people who are vulnerable do not have these support systems to fall back on. Myron Magnet in his book *The Dream and the Nightmare* talks about these self-indulgent ideas being invented by the haves only to be inflicted on the have-nots.[4] What we call the underclass is in part made up of the victims not only of a changing economy but also of a changing culture that they did not invent, cannot explain, and are powerless to resist.

This cultural shift helps explain the worldwide rise in crime. Let me compare two periods in English history—that before Queen Victoria, roughly from 1820 to 1830, and that after her, roughly from 1890 to 1920. I speak of England, not the United States, only for reasons of historical evidence. England can be said to have a national criminal justice system and national criminal justice data in ways that the United States does not. And I draw on the splendid book by Martin Wiener, *Reconstructing the Criminal*.[5]

In the first period, 1820 to 1830, Englishmen noticed that crime was rising in part because young men were moving to the cities and off the farms and getting into trouble. Gin was easily affordable. Women of doubtful reputation prowled the streets. Pickpockets were everywhere. People were beginning to drink to excess. England responded by a series of changes that had in common one theme, that of individual responsibility. These changes included the following: A professional police force was created that would try to hold individuals accountable for their actions. The reach of the law was widened, and behavior once ignored—vagrancy, prostitution, and public drunkenness—was now criminalized. This was done, not because anyone thought that a single vagrant, a single prostitute, or a single public drunk was a serious threat to society, but because they thought that regularizing the habits of everyone, even in small ways, was the necessary first step to regularizing their habits in large ways.

The brutality of punishments was dramatically lessened, capital punishment was abandoned save for a few offenses, and the horrible tortures that had been so characteristic (in theory if not in practice) of seventeenth- and eighteenth-century England were given up. Punishment was made more certain by reducing the range of excuses that people could offer to the magistrate if someone was arrested for a given offense. And finally, people spoke candidly and in public about the difference between reputable and disreputable persons. Those who spoke this way wished to emphasize the relevance of behavior and character over class and group. For any given status, one ought to distinguish carefully between those who are decent and those who are indecent.

As a consequence of these and other changes, crime went down in England. It went down in the United States also, and as a consequence, I believe, of similar changes in most of the states in this country. And that happened despite increasing urbanization, increasing immigration, and the advent of industrialization. All of those forces which to the modern mind seem to be the causes of crime were in the second half of the nineteenth century in England and the United States irrelevant to crime. The moral order had been strengthened, in part by public measures—the police, the new criminal law—but in part also by the proliferation of voluntary associations, temperance societies, YMCAs, mother aid societies, and child care societies aimed at controlling what people thought was the excessively impulsive nature of some human characters.

By the second period, from 1890 to 1920, the attitude had dramatically changed. It was a period of relatively low crime rates. In part because the problem seemed less severe and in part because elite opinion now drew on very different premises, policies toward crime in England, and I believe in the United States as well, also changed. During this period the reach of the criminal law was reduced. Vagrancy, drunkenness, and prostitution began to be decriminalized. The power of the police to investigate was narrowed and the number of defenses against conviction was widened. These new defenses included pleas of insanity, diminished responsibility, and youthful status. Elites stopped using the logic of individual accountability and started using the logic of social causation, and they began to abandon the distinction between the reputable and the disreputable poor.

These changes acquired their largest form in the 1960s, but they didn't begin there. Because the new premises were already in place, we were intellectually unprepared to cope with the sudden increase in crime that began in the early 1960s. And as a result, from the middle 1960s to the end of the 1970s the serious crime rate here and abroad increased dramatically. In every industrialized nation of the world except for Japan and Switzerland, this was a period of rapidly rising crime rates to which the intellectual response was generally the same: we must attack the "root causes."[6]

Let me give you some examples. In 1960 in this country the typical burglary committed by an adult resulted in fifty days in prison. By "fifty days in prison" I mean that for every burglary, the combined probability of the burglar being arrested, convicted, and imprisoned, multiplied by the average time served for all burglars, is a price of fifty days in prison. By 1980 that price tag had fallen to fifteen days in jail, a decline of two-thirds. That pattern remained the same throughout most of the 1970s. In the 1980s we began to reverse this. We began to restore some parity between the commission of a crime and the probability of punishment. Partly because of this, in 1980 the crime rate in the United States began to go down, and except for teenage violence it has more or less continued to go down ever since. England and Sweden followed a different policy. They allowed the prison price of burglary to go down during the 1980s, and partly as a result of this policy their property crime rate continued to go up. [7]

But prison price tags are not the whole story. The average American knows that even under the best of conditions most crimes will go unpunished and many children will turn to crime before they know of its costs. And because of the vast cultural shifts we have experienced, we can never hope to return to the low crime rates of the 1950s. In 1986, despite the enormous investment in police departments, prosecutions, and prison cells, the average number of days in jail for a typical burglary committed by an adult in this country had only got back up to twenty-one—still less than half of what it was in 1960.[8] Moreover, the increase in prosperity and the advent of a consumerist society have made it much easier and more tempting to steal things. We now have self-service stores; some people take that a bit more literally than we intend. Banks used to be imposing Greco-Roman fortresses located downtown and surrounded by guards and bars. Today banks are in a shopping mall or inside a supermarket and conveniently near the freeway exit. We do not wish to sacrifice freedom and prosperity, even in the name of crime control. And we should not. But, some may ask, cannot we reverse, or at least moderate, the impact on crime (and drug abuse, illegitimacy, and public disorder) of our culture of radical individualism and self-indulgence?

That culture was not the result of government action and cannot be changed by new government policies. We all know that the family is weaker as a socializing influence, but it is not obvious that the government made it weaker or can now make it stronger. How should we think about the position of the family? I don't think we can make a meaningful difference by changing marginal tax rates. I don't think we change the family by having a national family policy. I don't think we change the family by mandatory parenting courses taught in all the schools. After all, mankind has survived for many millennia without the benefit of Dr. Spock, much less parenting classes in junior high school for pregnant girls.

But there is one area where we do directly confront the family, and that is welfare policy. We know that children, white or black, raised in single-parent families at any income level save the very highest are more at risk for all kinds of emotional and social problems than are children raised in two-parent families.[9] Now whatever you may think is the cause of the rise of single-parent families, the welfare system puts people in a relationship with their government and society that is radically individualistic. It says, in effect, that if you, at age sixteen, get pregnant and have no man who will marry you and help you raise your child, we the government will send you a check, food stamps, and housing vouchers and make you eligible for Medicaid. You will get these benefits as an individual, and you will decide how to use these resources, even at age sixteen or fifteen. You can stay in school and we will set aside a day care room where your children can be parked while you attend school. The children who grow up in that environment are greatly at risk for repeating that cycle. Welfare dependency has become an intergenerational phenomenon. Suppose we change the terms of that trade. Suppose we say, "If you apply as an underage girl for welfare, housing assistance, and food stamps because you have given birth and are unmarried, we will not give the money to you, we will give it to some family with which you must live. That family might be your own family, it might be someone else's family, or it might be a family shelter or group home run by some private association." The goal is to give to the girl, but above all to give to her child, a sense of what it's like to grow up in a real family surrounded by real adults who will shelter them from the mean streets and equip them with expectations about the importance of work and family.

I think that if we redefine the welfare reform debate to be a debate about how we save a lost generation of children, we would understand more clearly what our priorities ought to be. We would like to reduce illegitimacy but we don't know how. We would like to save money, but money is not the fundamental issue. If we spent all that money and got something for it, most people would be willing to spend it. Some people want mothers to work, but do we want young mothers with children only two or three years old to work? What we really want to do is alter the life prospects of those children who have been put at risk because of this long-term cultural change, this destigmatization of out-of-wedlock births, and this delegitimization of family values.

Would such a policy help moderate the effects of the new self-indulgent culture? I do not know. But such a policy requires of us nothing that we have not tried before, albeit on a small scale. The Florence Crittenden Homes have been providing shelters for unwed mothers for decades. The Saint Martin DePorres Home in Chicago, run by Sister Connie Driscol, is doing it today, but with private money. Perhaps if government money touched such enterprises, they would lose their value, because with government dollars come government rules.

My purpose is not to persuade you that this is the right policy; it is only to persuade you that we ought to try some feasible policies that will redefine the relationship between vulnerable people and an individualized society. We have to make them understand that this society, like all other viable societies in the history of the world, was based on two-parent families. The cultural experimentation that began in the 1890s, that began to acquire widespread acceptance in the 1920s, and that finally came to full flower in the 1960s has exacted a price for the benefits it has conferred.

Notes

1. John Stuart Mill, *On Liberty*, ed. David Spitz (New York: W. W. Norton, 1975), 10-11.

2. John Stuart Mill, *Essays on Politics and Culture*, ed. Gertrude Himmelfarb (New York: Anchor Books, 1963), 14.

3. Lytton Strachney, *Eminent Victorians: Cardinal Manning, Florence Nightingale, Dr. Arnold, and General Gordon*, (New York: G. P. Putnam's Sons, 1918).

4. Myron Magnet, *The Dream and the Nightmare* (New York: William Morrow, 1993).

5. Martin Wiener, *Reconstructing the Criminal* (Cambridge: Cambridge University Press, 1990).

6. Mark A. R. Kleiman, "Imprisonment to Offense Ratios," paper no. 89-0602 (J. F. Kennedy School of Government, Harvard University: August 5, 1988).

7. Ibid.

8. Ibid.

9. *Family Structure and Children's Health: United States*, series 19, no. 78 (National Center for Health Statistics, U.S. Department of Health and Human Services, 1988).

2

Family, Fatherhood, and Socialization

Don E. Eberly

My topic is the role of family in the socialization process, but I want to tie the topic to a broader concern for the condition of our democracy and the state of civil society in America.

We Americans are increasingly having to confront what may be the most painful paradox of human history. As a nation we are more free and more prosperous than any in history. We have been great at entrepreneurship. We have been great at science. Our accomplishments in technological innovation are staggering. Even with its faults, our democratic system is the best ever devised. We have done all of these things as well as any nation in history. For the first time since American-style democracy was born, no serious rival to democratic capitalism exists around the world.

And yet in the midst of this remarkable progress, all is not well. Why, in the midst of all of these accomplishments, are Americans frowning? Why are anxiety, cynicism, and distrust so pervasive today regardless of policy change in Washington? America spent decades applying her strength abroad confronting the forces of aggression only to become increasingly defenseless against the forces of social decomposition at home.

And so we must confront this paradox: We, the unrivaled military leader in the world and the undisputed economic heavyweight of the world, increasingly lead the Western world in many categories of social dysfunction. Among our distinctions—the highest divorce rate, the highest teen pregnancy rate, the highest child poverty rate.

What we are experiencing is fairly widespread social regression. Social regression reflects a real decline in our social institutions, especially the family, a weakening of citizenship, and an erosion of the psychological and spiritual strength that a free society and democracy depend upon to function well. What compounds this social regression is the fact that it may be largely unaffected by the other leading revolutions—policy devolution and information revolution—that are producing so many breakthroughs for society. Social factors are inevitably dependent on human behavior and not on systems and structures (for example, welfare and education) which can be reformed.

Much of the anxiety in this country has to do with the condition of society—there is a generalized sense that the fabric of our communities is weakening and that our public and private institutions are burdened down with conflicts and seemingly intractable problems. How sufficient, many are asking, is economic advancement, if our schools do not function, crime defies control, and our children lose their innocence in an adversarial culture of coarseness, violence, and banality.

We would like very much to believe that we have wrong-headed politicians and flawed policies to blame for what has come to pass. We especially try to console ourselves by supposing that these conditions came about mostly through the rise of the welfare state and the conduct of poor people. Yet ill-conceived state policies are not remotely capable of producing the scale of out-of-wedlock births, divorce, father absence and general criminality that now exists. These are societal problems, and they originate predominantly in the collapse of character-shaping institutions.

One now observes a rather profound and welcome shift in the national debate. Many intellectuals and journalists are steadily joining what Jean Elshtain calls the "ranks of the nervous." There is a growing sense that, as Elshtain states, "our democracy is faltering," that it is "succumbing to exhaustion, cynicism, opportunism."[1] If democracy is faltering, it is because civil society is faltering.

When civil society declines, we are forced to encounter a decline not just in actual civility, but in the capacity of individuals to regulate the self and transcend the self by acting with genuine respect for the preferences and welfare of others. A society that is well-ordered, civil, and humane is one in which large percentages of individuals pass successfully through childhood into adulthood having acquired the capacity for the regulation of impulses.

So there is a far greater sense today of what is missing, what is lacking, and what we seem to want. Americans now seem to want a lot more character and restraint, more respect and responsibility. But while people seem to want these things, it is far less clear that they have any idea where what they now want comes from, and even less clear that they are willing to pay any personal price to get it by trading off many of the boundless individual freedoms they have recently acquired. More consequential than any other cultural change has been the rise of the autonomous self and the triumph of the ethos of self-expression.

Knowing what we want will do little, by itself, to assure that we get what we want. We must ask ourselves, again and again, where does the capacity to live a self-governed life come from? It comes from functioning institutions, starting with family, religion, and voluntary associations. Society is capable of enduring painful economic dislocation, natural calamity, and war if foundational institutions are strong, as we learned during the period of depression and war in the early twentieth century. If the institutions are weak, society atrophies, even during times of prosperity.

It is in this context, then, that I want to address the family, and especially fatherhood—as institutions that fundamentally shape the character of individuals and their competence for democratic life. In order to rebuild society, the moral claims of family and of community must once again hold greater sway over the individual.

Few would argue with the basic contention that the family is the primary socializing agency. That is very easy to acknowledge. It is important to point out, however, that "family" has become a highly elastic term. In some quarters it means little more than a collection of adults bound together by some temporary need. This relativization of the family fits comfortably with the broadly felt desire among adults to justify the dramatic expansion of what in recent times has been termed lifestyle choices. The entrance of pluralistic language into the discussion of the family reflects broad societal accommodation of a steep rise in separated, divorced, blended, and never formed families led by young mothers. The pluralistic definition of family excludes no one and thus the term "family" has been stripped of most of its meaning. It is a term indistinguishable from the term "household."

Why does this matter? The immediate consequence of relativization of family is to write fathers entirely out of the family script. When the cutting and pasting begins on the ever changing family portrait, it is the father that is casually blotted out. In the vast majority of cases, children from fragmented families live apart from their biological father. The reinvention of the family rests entirely upon society's acceptance of one basic myth: that fathers are superfluous; that they play no unique, gender-specific role in raising children and are thus replaceable; and that children will do just fine without them.

The modern cultural script, then, commonly portrays the father, as frequently as not, as an extra set of hands, a deputy mom, a provider of a child support payment, more akin to a relative than a devoted, nurturing father. Not infrequently dad is seen as a dunce or, worse yet, an ever-present danger. Of all the statistical distortions that have been circulated about the American family, there is none more egregious than the frequent suggestion that married men are the source of most abuse of women and children. The data, in reality, confirm our basic intuition, which is that fatherhood in the context of marriage is the chief inhibitor of male aggression. Married women and their children are far less likely to face physical abuse than women and children in households where boyfriends drift in and out under tenuous and unstable conditions.

Reasserting a basic family norm of two parents, preferably the biological parents, hinges upon the case I wish to make for the unique and irreplaceable role of the father. The worry has never been that mothers, in tending to the welfare of children, might fall short in fulfilling their biologically determined role—this has never occurred broadly across time and human societies. The case for family restoration, and improving child welfare, rests almost entirely on whether, in fact, fathers are unique and irreplaceable and should thus be expected by society to carry out a role less biologically determined than that of mothers but nevertheless vital to children. If fathers are disposable and replaceable, then the current expanded definition of family is justified—we might even want to expand it further.

The Nature of Father Absence

Many will ask, why all of this sudden interest in father absence? Societies, including our own, have always had a certain percentage of father absence in various forms: Fathers have always left the home for work or war, sometimes for long periods of time, often never returning. Moreover, we have always had a certain amount of divorce and a certain amount of out-of-wedlock births. And in all too many cases, dating back to the beginning of recorded human history, there have been fathers who have been largely dysfunctional—perhaps physically present, but in all other regards checked out. The family revisionists are correct at least in the limited sense that the family has always been under some stress. Family life, as young and old alike will attest, is difficult work.

The revisionists are wrong, however, in refusing to acknowledge that what American society is having to cope with today is radically different. Father absence is radically different in nature, as well as in scale, and it is these differences that must be understood as posing a unique threat to society.

In the nineteenth century the overwhelming source of father absence was death. By the 1960s the overwhelming majority of single-parent households were created by divorce or out-of-wedlock births. In other words, the form of father absence became voluntary or volitional. As David Blankenhorn, author of *Fatherless America*, puts it: death merely puts an end to the father; voluntary absence puts an end to fatherhood.[2]

The Scale of Father Absence

The father absence of today is also different, far different, in scale. America passed Sweden in 1986 for the dubious distinction of leading the world in father absence.[3] According to David Blankenhorn, fatherlessness is now approaching a rough parity with fatherhood as a defining feature of American childhood.

More than one-third of the nation's children will go to sleep in a home in which their fathers do not live. Half of all white children and 75 percent of all black children born today will spend at least some time before the age of eighteen living in a father-absent household.[4]

The number of children living only with their mother grew from 5.1 million in 1960 to 15.6 million in 1993. The percentage of children born out of wedlock is now slightly over 30 percent (68 percent of black, 36 percent of Hispanic, and 22 percent of white children) and rising rapidly, up from 5 percent in 1960.

According to some estimations, 40 percent of all American children, and 80 percent of minority children, will be born out of wedlock by the turn of the century.[5]

Some will say that it is somewhat arbitrary to define a father's presence or absence in the lives of his children by virtue of his street address. Many fathers who do not live with their biological offspring are conscientious and do quite well across the distance, and many more would prefer to do a better job but are prevented from doing so by discriminatory custody rulings, or by resistance from their children's mothers. But the data confirm what we often suspect about males, which is that they simply do not carry the same biological predisposition toward involved parenting as the mother. In fact, when men are removed from their children and their children's mother, what often follows is a great disappearing act.

More than one-half of all children who do not live with their father have never been in their fathers' homes. Forty percent of the children who live in fatherless households have not seen their fathers in at least a year. Of the remaining 60 percent only 20 percent spend even one night per month in the fathers' homes.[6]

While every father, whatever his circumstances, must be called upon to carry out the full range of his parenting responsibilities, any strategy that places too much confidence in structural remedies must be resisted. It is highly unlikely that the best and most rigorously enforced child support system, or the best custody laws, will do very much by itself to connect fathers to their children. Moreover, the last thing the children of America need is a new ideal of fatherhood that consists of dad sending his child support payment in on time.

The Consequences of Father Absence

Let me now call your attention to some of the details of this problem. There are few factors more consequential to children and to society than father absence. Although the correlation of father absence to all manner of personal difficulty and social maladjustment is pretty much a settled empirical question, the full dimensions of the problem rarely pass through the society's multiple media filters.

Time does not permit a discussion of all facets of father absence, but they are many. According to prominent psychologist Urie Bronfenbrenner, controlling for factors such as low income, children growing up in father-absent households

> are at greater risk for experiencing a variety of behavioral and educational problems, including extremes of hyperactivity and withdrawal; lack of attentiveness in classroom; difficulty in deferring gratification; impaired academic achievement; school misbehavior; absenteeism; dropping out; involvement in socially alienated peer groups; and the so-called "teenage syndrome" of behaviors that tend to hang together—smoking, drinking early and frequent sexual experience, and in the more extreme cases, drugs, suicide, vandalism, violence and criminal acts.[7]

Rather than spend a lot of time on all of these, let me just dwell on three that are of the greatest social and fiscal consequence to our nation: child poverty, the

AFDC caseload, and crime.

Father Absence and Child Poverty

It is humbling for the world's richest democracy to have a poverty rate twice that of any other industrial nation and to be singled out by international agencies as a world leader in child poverty and youth homicides. Whatever one's politics, each of us harbors as a human being a deep desire to see suffering and deprivation among children reduced. If there is a common aspiration among all of us, this would be it. What few realize is just how close our society's performance would have come to matching its promise had we not changed our mind about marriage and family.

If we had simply done a better job as a society of preventing the creation of father-absent households, we would today have a society far more just, fair, and humane. Much of the rise in child poverty and much of the rise in the AFDC caseload correlate directly with the rise of father-absent households. According to Isabel Sawhill, "the rapid growth in the number of children living in single-parent families can explain virtually all of the growth in poverty among children since 1960."[8]

Whatever doubt may linger in elite minds about the unique socializing function of adult males, there can be no doubt about the economic consequences of their absence. According to David Ellwood, the vast majority of children who are raised entirely in a two-parent home will never be poor during their childhoods. By contrast, the vast majority of children who spend time in a single-parent home will experience poverty at some point in their lives.[9] According to a report issued by the Annie Casey Foundation, of the children whose mothers waited until they graduated from high school, turned twenty, and got married to have their first child, only 8 percent experienced poverty, compared to 79 percent of children whose mothers failed to do those three things.[10]

The disappearance of fathers as income earners from the family over the past thirty years has dramatically altered the face of poverty. The term "feminization" of poverty best describes the impact of these changing trends. In 1960, 29 percent of poor families were headed by women; today 60 percent of all poor households are female-headed. In 1960, two-thirds of the heads of poor families worked; in 1992, only 49 percent worked at all, and only 15 percent worked year long. In 1992, households in poverty were characterized by fewer men, less work, less economic viability, and more socialization of income support for the family.[11]

Without detracting from the courage and character of the majority of single mothers, these households are not economically viable. Forty-seven percent of mother-only households are poor, compared to 8 percent in which mother and father are present. Almost 75 percent of American children living in single-parent families will experience poverty before they turn eleven years old, compared to 20 percent of children in two-parent households.[12]

The tendency of social policy experts will be to dwell upon programs to ameliorate the economic stress of these households. But the idea that we can close the gap through governmental structures is truly a pipe dream. Even the boldest and costliest experiments in child support enforcement have produced disappointing results. According to family scholar David Blankenhorn, America now employs thirty thousand people in the child support enforcement system, and little progress has been made in improving child welfare. The best system has nothing to offer in the growing number of cases where either paternity is not established, court orders do not exist, or mothers do not seek the fathers' financial support because they do not want the fathers of their children in their lives. To illustrate the point, consider that the fastest-rising category of single-parent household is the so-called single-mother-by-choice category.

AFDC Caseload

Over 50 percent of all new welfare cases are due to births to unmarried women, many of them teens. Space does not permit full discussion, but these households are the most marginal of all, and most consequential to society. Two-thirds of unwed mothers are poor and three-fourths go on welfare. Almost half of unwed teen mothers go on welfare within one year of their baby's birth. By the time their first baby is five years old, 72 percent of white teens and 84 percent of black teens have received AFDC payments.[13]

We are well aware that policy reforms offering reduced incentives for out-of-wedlock births are in the works. This, of course, will help somewhat. But the evidence that this social pathogen has deeper roots is strong, and it should temper our enthusiasm for policy reforms absent broader societywide changes in how we treat single motherhood, especially among teens.

Studies indicate that children born out of wedlock are dramatically more likely to bear children out of wedlock, with or without the encouragement of an AFDC check. Daughters raised in father-absent households are 164 percent more likely to have a premarital birth, 111 percent more likely to give birth as a teenager, and far more likely (92 percent) to dissolve a marriage if it does form.[14]

Crime

The most dangerous consequence of father absence is the rise of crime and disorder, which is aimed like a dagger at the heart of society. The factor which is most destructive of civil society and democratic order is the fear and distrust resulting from broad and poorly controlled criminality. Neighborhoods and private associations do not function well when the overriding objective of many citizens is to simply secure safety.

Once again, before we can make headway toward a safer society, we must look more closely at the roots of this crime. Who is committing crime? Crime is still overwhelmingly committed by males, and overwhelmingly by males not properly fathered. In 1965, Daniel Patrick Moynihan said "a community that allows a large number of young men to grow up in broken homes, dominated by women, never acquiring any stable relationship to male authority, never acquiring any rational expectations about the future—that community asks for and gets chaos."[15]

Poorly socialized males have been a problem for human civilization from the beginning of time. There is a two-sided problem in male socialization: one is the separation of children from fathers, and the other is separation of fathers from children. There is the problem of the unfathered child, and there is the equally consequential problem of the unattached male.

Almost a quarter of all men under the age of thirty-four live in nonfamily households, either as singles or with unattached others.[16] As columnist David Broder captured it: "Every society must be wary of the unattached male, for he is universally the cause of numerous social ills. The good society is heavily dependent on men being attached to a strong moral order centered on families, both to discipline their sexual behavior and to reduce their competitive aggression."[17]

Studies indicate that the chief predictor of violent crime and burglary in a community is the proportion of father-absent households. We have seen over the past decade an explosion in adolescent crime. Seventy percent of the inmates in juvenile reform institutions and 72 percent of the adolescents serving sentences for murder are from father-absent households.[18]

Father presence or absence is *the* independent variable on the issue of crime. According to a study released by the Progressive Policy Institute, the relationship between family structure and crime is so strong that controlling for family configuration erases the relationship between race and crime and between low income and crime.[19] This relationship, the study says, turns up again and again in the literature.

If we want to understand crime and, more importantly, if we want to do something about crime, we must understand what dads do to guide male aggression toward pro-social activity—toward self-control, toward the management of conflict, and toward the respect of women. As pointed out earlier, women and children are at substantially higher risk of physical and sexual abuse in disrupted households. Sixty-two percent of all rapists were raised in single-parent households.

Causes

What explains the nature and scale of this phenomenon? How did it come to pass? The explanations that are most frequently offered are typically structural in nature. They focus on industrialization, which separated male breadwinning from the home and farm; the rise of mobility; and the decline in small-bounded face-to-face communities where extreme individualism was countered by the maintenance of moral standards and reciprocal obligations. More recently the emphasis has turned to stagnating male wages especially for urban males, and specifically to the transition from a manufacturing economy, which tended to favor males, to an information-based economy that may favor women. Still others cite the decline in male dominance in the role of breadwinning generally. All of these possess some validity, of course.

I will offer my own explanation, which is predominantly rooted in cultural and moral, not economic or structural, explanations. After all, human society has always been advancing through periods of economic dislocation and social disruption, but never before have we experienced this scale of father absence.

Fatherhood is basically a cultural institution. Fathering, says sociologist John Miller, is "a cultural acquisition to an extent that mothering is not." Given that there are few biologically compelling reasons for the male to care for his offspring, "a set of overlapping largely cultural developments" is required. When a culture "ceases to support a father's involvement with his own children (through its laws, mores, symbols, models, rituals) powerful natural forces take over in favor of the mother-only family." The father-involved family, Miller says, "must be viewed as the definitive cultural artifact that lies at the foundation of all other cultural achievements and most uniquely distinguishes what it means to be human from other forms of life."[20]

If fatherhood is culturally acquired, not biologically conditioned, how do we get out of this? Of course, there are economic incentives that will help. There are policy reforms that will contribute. But the restoration of fathers to their children will happen when an all-fronts mobilization takes place within society to reinforce adult male responsibility for children.

Periodically, widespread fear of disorder and a loathing of the appalling disregard of social standards and obligations have produced a rapid shift away from expressive values toward constraint and obligation. The pattern of loosening social mores and softening definitions of deviance is reversed. In the case of father absence, the disappearance of fathers from children once more produces at least a gentle but firm social opprobrium.

Aiding in this renewal may be broader social reform currents emphasizing character and self-control. James Q. Wilson cites the work of Joseph F. Kett, who has traced various social reform movements that have come along aiming to uplift moral standards.[21] They had a common desire to instill character, which meant once more treating the individual as capable of and responsible for inner control. Social ills were confronted by recovering a self-activating, self-regulating, all-purpose inner control.

This approach best fits the American pattern of social change and renewal. What is needed to save families, to make neighborhoods friendly and safe, and to restore lost virtues are the dynamic social movements that have come along periodically in history. In the nineteenth century, for example, society witnessed an explosion of voluntary associations and organizations aimed at social reform and moral uplift. Spiritual awakenings, temperance movements, and many private and public efforts were made to strengthen character and responsibility. These were dynamic social movements that transcended politics and partisanship.

The renewal of fatherhood and the renewal of civil society may go hand in hand. Wilson says that "throughout history, the institutions that have produced effective male socialization have been private, not public." If this is true, he says, "then our policy ought to be to identify, evaluate and encourage those local, private efforts that seem to do the best job at reducing drug abuse, inducing people to marry, persuading parents, especially fathers, to take responsibility for their children, and exercising informal social controls over neighborhood streets."[22]

Margaret Mead predicted on her deathbed that the survival of civilization will depend, not on governments and bureaucracies, but on "citizen volunteer associations, gathering together, deepening and growing together, and going out and taking social action."

Notes

1. Jean Bethke Elshtain, *Democracy on Trial* (New York: Basic Books, 1995), xvii.

2. David Blankenhorn, *Fatherless America: Confronting Our Most Urgent Social Problem* (New York: Basic Books, 1995), 23.

3. Wade F. Horn, *Father Facts* (Lancaster, Pa. National Fatherhood Initiative, 1995), 3.

4. Ibid., 3.

5. Ibid., 3, 12, 14.

6. Ibid., 20.

7. Ibid., 30.

8. Richard T. Gill and T. Glandon Gill, *Family Affairs* (Newsletter of the Institute for American Values in New York City) 6, nos. 1–2 (Winter 1994), 2.

9. D. T. Ellwood, *Poor Support: Poverty in the American Family* (New York: Basic Books, 1988).

10. *Kids Count Data Book* (Annie E. Casey Foundation, 1995).

11. Lawrence Mead, "The Politics of Welfare Reform," in *Policy Visions* (Center for Economic and Policy Education) 1, no. 4 (August 1994).

12. *Father Facts*, 41.

13. *The Green Book*, U.S. Congress Committee on Ways and Means (Washington D.C., 1994).

14. *Father Facts*, 16.

15. Ibid., 1.

16. David Popenoe, "The Family Condition of America," in *Values and Public Policy*, ed. Henry Aaron, Thomas Mann, and Timothy Taylor (Washington: Brookings Institution, 1994), 98.

17. David Broder, *Washington Post*, 16 February 1994.

18. *Father Facts*, 24.

19. Elaine Kamarck and William Galston, "Putting Children First: A Progressive Family Policy for the 1990s" (Washington D.C.: Progressive Policy Institute, September, 1990).

20. John Miller, *Biblical Faith and Fathering: Why We Call God Father* (New York: Paulist Press, 1989), Chapters 1 and 2.

21. James Q. Wilson, "Culture, Incentives, and the Underclass," in *Values and Public Policy*, ed. Henry Aaron, Thomas Mann, and Timothy Taylor (Washington: Brookings Institution, 1994), 54.

22. Ibid., 74.

3

Values and Judgments: Creating Social Incentives for Good Behavior

Glenn C. Loury

A Discourse on Virtue

Though I am a social scientist, I confess to being pessimistic that social science can ultimately contribute much to the resolution of the profound social ills of poverty, despair, and decay evident in the core central cities of this country. This is not to disparage the often ingenious efforts that social scientists employ to fathom the intricacies of human behavior. Still, I question whether real change in the lives of real people depends much at all on answers to the kinds of questions that social scientists pose.

Why this skepticism? Because modern social science speaks a language of cause and effect—"if we design this program then they will respond in that way." Yet I am now convinced that the core social problems of our time require for their solution a language of values—"we *should* do this; they *ought* to do that; decent people *must* strive to live in a certain way." This is the language of the pulpit, not the conference room. In the discourse of the "policy wonk," who speaks fluent "conference-ese," there is no place for language like this.

Yet we know that our most serious social problems are connected with dysfunctional behaviors adopted by young people in our various communities. As a number of critics[1] have emphasized recently, there is a relationship between the behavioral problems of the poor and the cultural crisis affecting the middle and upper classes in America, as evidenced by rising divorce rates, the spread of venereal disease, the problems of our education system, increases in teen suicide, alcohol and drug abuse, our problems in international competitiveness, our flight from responsibility into various therapies which stress our victimhood, and so forth.

At issue here is our capacity as a moral and political community to engage in an effective discourse about values and ways of living, and to convey normative judgments which arise out of that discourse. I am dubious about the ability of modern political rhetoric to rise to the challenge which such a "discourse on virtue" poses to public figures. Consider the collective guffaw with which much influential opinion received the promotion of "family values" in the last presidential campaign. This was not just partisanship; it was a contemptuous rejection of the very idea of a public discourse which might judge how we should organize our family lives.

This is an interesting situation, for judgment is not unknown in our public discourses. National campaigns have, indeed, been waged, aimed at some aspects of behavior, with positive results. Smoking is the obvious example, successfully inveighed against over the last generation, with both public and private efforts. Our national consciousness of environmental issues has been raised in recent decades, in part through the use of public rhetoric and exhortation which has had a powerful normative aspect to it. One only need read Al Gore's book *Earth in the Balance* to see that.[2] But efforts at public exhortation about sexuality, marriage, and childbearing are far more contentious because, unlike in these other areas, such efforts cut against the ideological grain of the great "liberation" movements which have swept through our society in past decades. Even some conservative Republican presidential candidates are reluctant to engage in public rhetoric with a direct moral message. This should tell us something about the limits of politics as a means of addressing profound questions of value.

The Limits of Economic Determinism

Another reason to be skeptical about the utility of social science is that its fundamental behavioral assumptions begin from a materialist viewpoint. Economic or biological factors are supposed ultimately to underlie all behavioral problems, even behaviors involving sexuality, marriage, childbearing, and parenting which reflect people's basic understandings of what gives meaning to their lives. The view is that these behavioral problems can be cured from without, that government can change these behaviors, that if you can just get the incentives right, then everything will be fine. This reflects a philosophy of mechanistic determinism, wherein the mysteries of human motivation are supposedly susceptible to calculated intervention, if only the government were sufficiently committed to try.

Yet there is another view, illustrated by the carpenter from Galilee who reminded his tempter, "Man does not live by bread alone, but by every word that proceedeth out of the mouth of God." And to the biological determinist, whom Christ does not address directly in the Gospels, one readily imagines he would say something like "God is not finished with us when he deals us our genetic hand."

But such an emphasis cuts against the modern sensibility. Deterministic views of social disorder lend themselves easily to the favored lines of partisan argument about social policy. Those who favor expanded government can argue that we either pay now for social "investment" programs, or pay later for welfare and prisons. Those who want the federal budget to shrink can cite the worsening conditions of the ghetto in the face of the growth in social spending over the last generation as evidence that the Great Society failed. Those who seek a middle way can split the difference by talking about how the receipt of benefits must be accompanied by an acceptance of responsibility on the part of the poor, though the government must provide services which help the poor to accept their responsibilities and so on. We are all familiar with this language.

These debates are sterile and superficial. They fail to engage questions of personal morality. They fail to talk about character and values. They do not invoke any moral leadership in the public sphere. The view seems to be that in a pluralistic society such discussions from public officials are inappropriate.

I am reminded here of a distinction introduced by the economist Albert Hirschman between tastes, defined as individual preferences about which we do not argue (e.g., whether we like apples or pears), and values, defined as preferences over which we do argue, both with ourselves and with others. We do not, for example, treat a preference for discrimination against blacks or women as a taste to be accommodated. Rather, we attempt to persuade, cajole, or compel our fellows to make "progress" in such areas, and we insist that our educational institutions instill in our young the "proper" views concerning them. Values, in other words, are personal preferences so central to our collective lives that as a political community we cannot properly be neutral about them. As Hirschman has noted: "A principal purpose of publicly proclaimed laws and regulations is to stigmatize antisocial behavior and thereby to influence citizens' values and behavior codes."[3]

Do we teach in our schools the comparative virtues of alternative ways of living? We give only muted public voice to the judgments that it is wrong to be sexually promiscuous, to be indolent and without discipline, to be disrespectful of legitimate authority, or to be unreliable or untruthful or unfaithful. We no longer teach values, but offer "clarification" of the values that the children are supposed to have somehow inculcated in them without any instruction. We elevate process ("How does one discover his or her own values?") over substance ("What is it that a decent person should embrace?"). The advocacy of a particular conception of virtuous living has virtually vanished from American public discourse. Who will say that young people *should* abstain from sexual intimacy until their relationships have been consecrated by marriage? These are, in this present age, not matters for public discourse.

Most Americans believe that 1.5 million abortions a year are far too many, and that this constitutes a profound moral problem for our society.[4] Yet the public discourse on this issue is dominated by the question of a woman's right to choose, not the moral content of her choice. Nearly all of us would prefer, on moral as well as pragmatic grounds, that our fifteen-year-olds not be sexually active. But to take this stance in the face of an epidemic of sexually transmitted disease invites ridicule from the highest officials. Government, it would appear, should confine itself to dealing with the consequences of these moral lapses, rather than directly taking on the issue of morality.

Now, I am not one for tilting at windmills. The emergence of morally authoritative public leadership seems unlikely at this late date. We shall have to look to the private agencies of moral and cultural development in particular communities to take on the burden of promoting positive behavioral change. In every community there are such agencies which seek to shape the ways in which individuals conceive of their duties to themselves, of their obligations to each other, and of their responsibilities before God. The family and the church are primary among these.

These are the natural sources of legitimate moral teaching, which must be restored if the behavioral problems which afflict our society are to be overcome. Such a restoration obviously cannot be the object of programmatic intervention by public agencies. Rather, it must be led from within the communities in question, by the moral and spiritual leaders of those communities.

Values, Policy, and the State

Let me talk now, for a few moments, about the role of the state. Public policy is more than the implementation of technical solutions to the problems of governance. It is also a powerful symbolic mechanism through which are communicated the values and beliefs of a people. As George Will has famously put it: "Statecraft is soulcraft."[5] The means-end calculation of the social scientist or policy analyst is insufficient to provide a full account of what government does. Crucial also is the expressive content of government actions. The actions taken by Congress regarding welfare reform represent a powerful expression about the duties and obligations of citizens, and about the standards of conduct expected from individuals. These messages both shape and reflect the values of the citizenry.

It is now widely accepted that placing upon welfare recipients the obligation to engage in activities which limit their dependence is necessary and legitimate public policy. Far from being punitive, as some liberal critics of this proposal allege, the imposition of such obligation represents a keeping of faith with a social accord of mutual expectation. The key point to recognize is that the state cannot escape the necessity to communicate some moral message by the actions it takes, even if only by default. The failure to impose obligations on recipients is also an action, which signals what is valued in society.

The audience for these normative messages is not limited to the set of people directly affected, but extends to the entire population. Indeed, sustaining political support for public provision to the needy requires the maintenance of some compatibility between the values expressed through the policy and the beliefs broadly held by the public. The conduct of public policy also communicates something to the citizenry at large about the moral standing of those persons directly reached by policy. In the case of welfare, structuring assistance so that it leads to the eventual attainment of self-sufficiency by recipients actually shows respect for the subjects of state action, and enhances the dignity of these persons. By holding up a common standard of behavior to all citizens, we evidence our confidence that those who may now need our assistance are capable of becoming self-reliant. This avoids the situation in which "we" who are capable of responsible conduct and of generosity deign to provide for "them" who, by virtue of their dependency, are rendered objects of our concern, but are not treated as responsible moral agents. The notion that to treat the poor with dignity one must withdraw all constraint on the recipient and simply hand over the benefit unencumbered is in fact a contradiction. The absence of an enforced expectation that those in need will, in due course, join the self-supporting concedes that the needy are incapable of actions regarded as minimally expected of ordinary citizens—hardly a dignified posture.

The Importance of Civil Society
    Thus, in addition to providing direct economic incentives (via the tax code and through the design of programs providing financial benefits), the state sets the moral background within which civil society operates. But it is the civil sector of families, community organizations, churches, and various private philanthropic undertakings which must do the real work of promulgating and instilling values. The role of the state, while important in matters of public communication, is ultimately quite limited in matters of transforming the values of individual persons. One source of this limitation is the fact that encouraging "good behavior" intrinsically requires that discriminations be made among persons based on assessments that are difficult, legally and politically, for public agencies to make. After we have distinguished between right and wrong in public rhetoric, it becomes necessary in the concrete, ambiguous circumstances of everyday life to discern the extent to which particular individuals have risen to, or fallen short of, our expectations. That is, promoting virtue requires that standards be set and communicated, and that judgments be made as to whether those standards have been met. The making of such judgments requires knowledge about individual circumstances, and the drawing of distinctions between individual cases, which may exceed the capacity of public institutions. Because citizens have due process rights which cannot be fully abrogated, public judgments must be made in a manner which can be defended after the fact, and which carries a high burden of proof as to its legitimacy. Families and churches are not constrained to the same degree.
    Consider the difficulty of a state-sponsored agent making the judgment as to whether a welfare recipient has put forward adequate effort to prepare for and find

a job. The information available for this decision is generally limited to the observations of a social worker, and the self-report of the welfare recipient concerning her activities, together with a check on whether job interviews previously arranged have been pursued, and so on. Beyond this, very little information can be brought to bear. Action to limit the assistance due to a belief that the recipient was not trying hard enough might not stand up to subsequent judicial review. (Indeed, such actions might not be carried out by state employees who believed the obligations thereby imposed were not appropriate.) But, of course, families and communal groups providing help to the same individual would base their continued assistance, in part, upon just such information. They would discriminate more finely than a state-sponsored agent ever could between the subtle differences in behavior among individuals which constitute the real content of morality and virtue.

This point is especially critical when behavioral distinctions may have a disparate impact by race, and where charges of racial discrimination could arise. Anticipating these charges, public agents may withdraw from the degree of scrutiny of individual behavior which produced the racially disparate outcome. The fact is that the instruments available to public agents for the shaping of character are coarse and relatively indiscriminate, in comparison to the kinds of distinctions and judgments which people make in their private social lives all the time. Moreover, the ways in which a public agent can sanction individuals' dysfunctional behavior—withholding financial benefits primarily—may not be as compelling as the threat of social ostracism and peer disapproval which is readily available in private associations. The purpose of these observations is to caution against an overly optimistic assessment of the power of legislation to reverse the regrettable trends in the social behaviors of citizens.

It is also the case that state action is encumbered by the plurality of views as to what constitutes appropriate values in our society. The public morality reflected in state action is necessarily a "thin" conception of virtue, weak enough to accommodate the underlying diversity of value commitments amongst the various sectors of our society. This contrasts sharply with the "thick" conceptions of virtue characteristic of the moral communities in which we are embedded in private life. The conflict over sex education illustrates this point. Introducing into the public schools in any large city a curriculum of sex education that teaches the preferability of two-parent families might be resisted by educators who would cite the great number of their students from single-parent backgrounds. Yet it is arguable that these are the students most in need of hearing the authoritative expression of such value judgments. Of course, the same would not be true of sex instruction undertaken in a parochial school context.

My general proposition is that civil society and the state provide complementary inputs into the production of virtuous citizens. Legislators should look for ways to encourage virtue by encouraging the development and expansion of those private, voluntary associations within which the real work of character development is best done. Mutually concerned persons who trust one another enough to be able to exchange criticism constructively, establish codes of personal conduct, and enforce social sanctions against what is judged as undesirable behavior can create and enforce communal norms that lie beyond the capacity of the state to promulgate effectively. The coercion and resources of the state, though great, are not especially subtle.

Concerning the Black Community

Finally, I would like to discuss these ideas in relation to social problems affecting the black community in the United States. I want to consider just how the moral-ethical sensibilities of black Americans took root in the experience of slavery. My central point is easily stated: Enslaved persons were driven by brute circumstance to create among themselves a culture with spiritual and moral depth of truly heroic proportions. They simply had no choice. The brutality of the assault they endured—upon their persons, their relations one with another, and their sense of dignity and self-respect—was such that either they would be completely destroyed as moral beings, or they would find a way, through faith, to transcend their condition. As Alan Keyes puts it in his recent book, *Masters of the Dream*: "In effect, [the slaves] secured themselves against the depredations of a system devised to destroy their self-respect by storing their sense of personal worth in a form that made it hard to damage and hard to steal away."[6] Enslaved persons had to learn to transcend their material condition, or they would have been destroyed. That "man does not live by bread alone" was for them more than a theoretical proposition; grasping the truth of that proposition was their key to survival.

The Africans brought to America in bondage came to embrace the Christian faith, and to find in it the means of their moral salvation. A wealth of historical, theological, and cultural scholarship amply documents this claim. So do the surviving primary accounts, and the spirituals and "sorrow songs" of the slaves themselves. This Christian faith, and the relationship with God to which it gave rise, was fundamental to preserving a sense of worth and dignity among enslaved persons. Again quoting Keyes: it permitted "them to feel that they existed in and for themselves, rather than through their relationship with the enslavers."[7] Faith allowed those held permanently in bondage to avoid being consumed by their hatred, their despair, or their fear.

These moral and spiritual values, forged in what Herbert Storing once called "the school of slavery,"[8] proved to be profoundly significant in the postslavery development of black Americans. It was the emphasis on hard work, education, and decent living characteristic of the first generations of blacks after emancipation which made possible their considerable progress. A spirit of self-help, rooted in a deep-seated sense of self-respect, was widely embraced among blacks of all ideological persuasions, well into this century. They did what they did—educating their children, acquiring land, founding communal institutions, and struggling for equal rights—not in reaction to or for the approval of whites, but out of an internal conviction of their own worth and capacities. Even acts of black protest and expressions of grievance against whites were, ultimately, reflections of this inner sense of dignity. The crowning achievements of the civil rights movement—its nonviolent method and its successful effort at public moral suasion—can be seen as the projection into American politics of a set of spiritual values which had been evolving among blacks for over a century.

It is, therefore, with a sense of deep remorse that I must recount how, in the last generation, this ethos of self-reliance, moral rectitude, and unapologetic Christian piety has lost its place of primacy among black political, spiritual, and intellectual leaders. We have, indeed, fallen upon rather hard times. The ideological pre-suppositions of current black American political advocacy seem a world apart from the historic ethos which I just mentioned.   Some leaders, in civil rights organizations and the halls of Congress, are wedded to a conception of the black condition, and a method of appealing to the rest of the polity, which undermines the dignity of our people.   They seek, it would seem, to make blacks into the conscience of America, even at the price of our souls.   Though it mocks the idea of freedom to hold that, as free men and women, blacks ought nevertheless to leave the determination of the normative framework of our communal life to the vicissitudes of government policy, this is precisely what has been done.   The rhetoric is: "It costs more to keep a young black man in jail for a year than it does to send him to Yale for a year"—as if the difference between him being in jail or at Yale is a matter of the size of some bureaucrat's budget, rather than the behavior of the young man himself, and of those charged with his guidance and care.

What a historic abdication of responsibility is this posture among contemporary black political leadership, considering the blood that has been shed, the sacrifices that have been made, the determination, commitment, and dedication that have been shown by blacks of previous generations.   While black youngsters in the ghettos murder each other, poison their bodies and their minds with drugs and promiscuous sex, and ignore their responsibilities to their children, their community, and their nation, there is no place in the political lexicon of black leaders for talk of values, morality, and virtue.   If we can quote the Bible's book of Amos in public, as Martin Luther King Jr. famously did: "Let justice roll down like waters and righteousness like a mighty stream,"[9] then why not also the passage in 1 Corinthians concerning sexual immorality, in which Paul states: "Do you not know that your body is the temple of the Holy Spirit, who is in you, whom you have received from God. You are not your own, you were bought with a price. Therefore, honor God with your body." Which of these biblical injunctions is more relevant to the contemporary behavioral crisis afflicting black America?

Today's black leaders have become ever-ready doomsayers, alert to exploit their people's suffering by offering it up to more or less sympathetic whites as justification for incremental monetary transfers. But this posture ignores the great existential challenge facing black America today. The challenge is that of taking control of our own futures by exerting the requisite moral leadership, making the sacrifices of time and resources, and building the needed institutions so that black social and economic development may be advanced. No matter how windy the debate becomes among white liberals and conservatives as to what should be done in the public sphere, meeting this self-creating challenge ultimately depends upon black action. It is to desecrate the memory of our enslaved ancestors to hold that, as free men and women, blacks ought nonetheless passively to wait for white Americans, of whatever political persuasion, to come to the rescue. A people who languish in dependency, while the means through which we might work toward our own advancement exist, have surrendered our claim to dignity, and to the respect of our fellow citizens. If we are to be a truly free people, we must accept responsibility for our fate, even when it does not lie wholly in our hands.

This is a point of genuine spiritual truth, but it is also a practical point with deep political implications. The fact is that promoting virtuous behavior amongst the black American poor is essential to achieving the political goals of more inclusive social policy and expanded opportunity for this population. Whites do not need to be shown how to fear black youths in the cities, which is implicitly the view of advocates who threaten "long hot summers" if jobs programs and affirmative action are not expanded. Instead, whites must be taught how to respect and how to love these youngsters. An effective, persuasive black leadership must project the image of a disciplined, respectable black demeanor. That such comportment is not inconsistent with protest for redress of grievance is a great legacy of the civil rights movement. But more than disciplined protest is required. Discipline, orderliness, and virtue in every aspect of life will contribute to creating an aura of respectability and worth. Such an aura is a valuable political asset, and the natural byproduct of living one's life in a dignified, civilized manner.

Because racial oppression tangibly diminishes its victims, in their own eyes and in the eyes of others, the construction of new public identities and the simultaneous promotion of self-respect are crucial tasks facing those burdened with a history of oppression. Without this, there can be no genuine recovery from past victimization. A leading civil rights advocate teaches young blacks the exhortation: "I *am* somebody." True enough. But the next and crucial question is "Just who are you?" The black youngster should be prepared to respond: Because I am somebody, I will not accept unequal rights. Because I am somebody, I will waste no opportunity to better myself. Because I am somebody, I will respect my body by not polluting it with drugs or promiscuous sex. Because I am somebody—in my home, in my community, in my nation—I will comport myself responsibly, I will be accountable, I will be available to serve others as well as myself. It is the doing of these fine things, not the saying of fine words, which proves that here *is* somebody to be reckoned with.

That is, whether or not the youngster is somebody has little to do with the color of his skin, and everything to do with the content of his character. This inner-city youngster is not on his own in his struggle to live a more virtuous, more righteous life. None of us are. God is our copilot in this, as in all of life's journeys. As Paul wrote to the Corinthians: "No temptation has seized you except what is common to man; but God is faithful, He will not allow you to be tempted beyond your ability, but when you are tempted He will provide a way out so that you can bear it." Let us tell the youngster about this good news, so he will look for that way out.

Notes

1. Critics such as Orando Patterson, Myron Magnet, and Cornel West. See Orlando Patterson's article on gender relations among black American, "Backlash," in *Transition Magazine*, No. 62 (1993). Also see Myron Magnet, *The Dream and the Nightmare: The Sixties Legacy to the Underclass* (William Morrow, 1993) and Cornel West, *Race Matters* (Beacon Press, 1994).

2. Al Gore, *Earth in the Balance: Ecology and the Human Spirit* (Houghton-Mifflin, 1992).

3. Albert Hirschman, "Against Parsimony: Three Easy Ways of Complicating Some Categories of Economic Discourse" in Chapter 6 of his collection *Rival Views of Market Society* (Harvard University Press, 1992).

4. See *The American Woman: 1994-95, Where We Stand*, ed. Cynthia Costello and Anne J. Stone (New York: W. W. Norton and Co., 1994), p. 208.

5. George Will, *Statecraft as Soulcraft: What Government Does* (Simon and Schuster, 1983).

6. Alan Keyes, *Masters of the Dream* (William Morrow, 1995), 23.

7. Ibid., 59.

8. Herbert J. Storing, *Toward a More Perfect Union: Writings of Herbert J. Storing* (American Enterprise Institute Press, 1995), 176.

9. Martin Luther King Jr., "A Letter from Birmingham City Jail," in Testament of Hope: the Essential Writings of Martin Luther King Jr., ed. James Melvin Washington (San Francisco: Harper and Row Publishers, 1986), Chapter 6, 297.

4

Ethnicity and Immigration

Linda Chavez

Immigration did not get the attention it deserves until quite recently. When speaking on the subject of immigration only two years ago, particularly in places which do not have a very large immigrant population, I felt as if I was talking about a subject that nobody cared about and very few people knew about.[1]

All that has changed, and has changed rather rapidly, in part because of the attention that the issue of immigration received in the 1994 elections. In California a measure called Proposition 187, which would deny government benefits to illegal aliens, was placed on the ballot through the initiative process. The measure received national attention and was the subject of heated debate. Although many people—including a number of conservatives, such as Bill Bennett, Jack Kemp, and myself—had great problems with it, the proposition was favored by many political leaders, including Governor Wilson of California, and was ultimately approved with 59 percent of the vote.

Proposition 187 focused on the question of illegal aliens, but had the effect of raising the entire issue of immigration to a national level. We have always thought of ourselves as an immigrant nation and we are very proud of that heritage. But our attitudes toward immigrants are not all that positive and, quite frankly, they never have been. Several recent polls measuring public attitudes toward immigrants offer an interesting irony. When asked about immigrants who came during the early part of this century, 59 percent of respondents said they were overwhelmingly good for the country. But when the question was whether immigrants coming here today are good for the country, 60 percent said no.

Although we do not have public opinion polls from 1910 or 1915, we do have a substantial historical record that shows the attitude towards those immigrants that many today think did great things for this country was not very positive at the time they were admitted. Why is that? During the Proposition 187 campaign, Mexican-American and Latino leaders in California said that what we were seeing was just traditional xenophobia and racism. They claimed that the reason people do not like immigrants today is that they are racially different. I think that reflects an ahistorical view. People are not aware that as different as the Mexican immigrants coming today seem from the general population, so did the Italians, the Poles, the Greeks, and the Jews that came in 1910 and 1915 seem every bit as alien to the population of the United States at that time.

Part of the reason Proposition 187 was so popular and got so much attention is that there is tremendous fear on the subject of illegal aliens specifically. According to some polls, about two-thirds of the American public believe that a majority of the immigrants who are in the United States today are here illegally. They are wrong. Although it is impossible to tell exactly how many illegal aliens are living in the United States, the Census Bureau estimates they number about 4 million, or about 20 percent of the total foreign-born population—certainly not a majority.

What are the facts of immigration today? Why is there so much concern? There are a number of people who think it is a matter of race. This group does not just include the activists opposed to Proposition 187. *Alien Nation*, a recent book by Peter Brimelow, takes the view that the problem with the immigrant flow today is that it is composed of a culture completely alien to the United States. Indeed, when you look at the numbers, there are big differences. The immigrants who came in the early part of this century were southern and eastern European. Many of the people who were already here, and who were descendants of people from the British Isles and from northern Europe, looked at these new arrivals and thought they were pretty different. However, these were Europeans nonetheless and the immigrants who are coming today are not.

Between 80 and 85 percent of all legal entrants come from just two regions of the world: Latin America and Asia. Immigrants, both legal and illegal, who entered the United States between 1980 and 1990 numbered roughly 10 million persons. In pure numbers, that is the largest group of immigrants we have ever had. Of course, the population of the United States is significantly larger today than it was in 1915 or 1870. If you compare the number of immigrants who are arriving to the size of the total population, the rate of immigration is only about one-third what it was during the peak immigration period of 1900 to 1920.

Most people are not terribly concerned about Asian immigrants, and with good reason. Asian immigrants tend to be better educated than native-born Americans and are more likely to have advanced degrees. Asians are overwhelmingly a highly skilled immigrant group. What does worry many people are Latin immigrants. There is a perception that the Latin immigrants are truly different, that somehow they are going to resist the melting pot, that they are never going to assimilate. And I must say that it is not just xenophobes who are out there promoting this view. It is not simply the people who are opposed to immigration that are saying

Latinos are different and cannot make it in the United States; the leaders of the Latin American community say this as well. Some of the civil rights leaders in the Latino community claim that Latinos are the poorest of the poor, the most disadvantaged, the least educated persons in this society, and that without massive infusions of government help they are not going to make it. In light of this rhetoric, can we blame the American public for being concerned about millions of people coming to this country poorly educated and unable to succeed in society without substantial expenditure of tax dollars? It seems reasonable to say that maybe we should not want so many of them. This rhetoric, especially coming from Latino activists, very much increases the fear about Latinos in our society.

A number of years ago I was invited to a debate on Latinos in the twenty-first century at Stanford University. My opponents in this debate included a former president of the League of United Latin American Citizens, a Pulitzer Prize–winning reporter from the *Los Angeles Times*, a tenured member of the faculty at Stanford, an assistant to the Republican governor of the state of California, and an assistant to the state senate majority leader in California. All of the panelists were Latinos. The audience were mostly students from Stanford and other Bay-area colleges, which are some of the most elite universities in the entire world. These kids looked very much like upper middle-class Americans, despite the fact that their coloring was more like mine. They looked very much like the sons and daughters of successful people.

During the debate I talked about how I thought Hispanics were in fact assimilating. Arnold Torres, my opponent, objected, going to the podium, striking his fist down and saying: "We cannot assimilate and we will not." Yet all around me I saw this clear evidence of assimilation. The debate itself was in English—surely a sign of how assimilated its participants were. This discrepancy between reality and perception made me want to research this issue at greater length. The result was my book *Out of the Barrio*. I had found that every time I debated these issues and talked about how much progress was being made, my opponents would start citing statistics showing higher dropout rates, lower earnings, and so on for Hispanics. What was most upsetting about these figures was that they showed no significant progress in decades.

I started college in 1966 at the University of Colorado, and in my four years as an undergraduate, I had exactly one other Mexican-American in classes with me. And yet today I look around at a sea of brown faces at prestigious universities. Why don't the statistics show this obvious progress? The problem is that the government publishes statistics in a way I consider disingenuous. The government publishes statistics about the Hispanic population in the aggregate, lumping everybody together. In the period from 1960 to 1990, there have been significant changes in the Latino population. In 1960, 85 percent of the Latinos living here were U.S.-born. Many of these people had been here for several generations. In 1990, however, roughly 50 percent of adult Latinos were foreign-born.

This makes a great deal of difference. When your aggregate statistics reflect a huge number of new immigrants who come here looking English, with low levels of education, and without the skills to be able to compete in a highly technological society, you will confuse the picture. It is the equivalent of taking the Jewish community of the lower east side of Manhattan in 1915 and assuming that what you saw in that statistical picture was going to remain the same for generations. And if you did take that picture, you would have seen a population that was not particularly well-educated and was quite poor and showed other signs of social disruption. That static picture, taken at that point in time, would provide no idea what progress would occur over time among the Jewish population in the United States. Yet just that kind of static picture of Hispanics is what demographers present all the time, with no attempt to understand what is really happening.

When you separate U.S.-born from foreign-born Hispanics, you get a very different picture. New immigrants are worse off, by far, than the Hispanic population in general and certainly the U.S. population. But over a period of time, these immigrants, like all other immigrants that come to this country, move up. Studies estimate that it takes fifteen to twenty years for a Mexican immigrant male to catch up in earnings with his Mexican-American counterpart, and after twenty years he actually begins to earn more than his U.S.-born counterpart. That has to do with the nature of immigrants and self-selection. Immigrants tend to be highly motivated and hard-working—they are risk takers or they would not be here.

The U.S.-born Hispanic population looks pretty much like the rest of America. High school graduation rates for second generation Mexican-American males are about 80 percent. Although these rates are not quite as good as those of non-Hispanic white men, 90 percent of whom graduate, the differences are not terribly great. Mexican-American males earn about 80 percent of what non-Hispanic whites do. That 20 percent differential is largely a result of differences in education. When you adjust for other factors such as region of residence, age, and experience, you essentially eliminate the differences in earnings between these two groups. In my view, the U.S.-born Hispanic population has made a lot of progress.

Another issue that worries many Americans is assimilation. Much of the concern about the Latino immigrants who are coming is the perception that they are never going to learn English, and that they do not want to learn it either. As it turns out, at least for the U.S.-born population, that is the farthest thing from the truth. A majority of third-generation Mexican-Americans living in the United States speak only English. They are like third-generation Italians, Greeks, Poles, and so forth. They have lost the language of their grandparents, and their language is now English. Another encouraging statistic related to assimilation is intermarriage. About one-third of young U.S.-born Hispanics marry non-Hispanic whites. When sociologists talk about assimilation, the most important factor is intermarriage, because, after all, the children of such couples are not exclusively members of either group.

Unfortunately, that is not the end of the story. If the immigrants who are coming here today were coming to the same kind of society that greeted earlier generations, then I think we could rest assured that everything was going to proceed as it should. The problem is that we now live in a nation that has a very different public policy with respect to immigrants. When immigrant children in the past went into school, there was no question but that they were going to learn English. They were expected to learn English as part of the process of being brought into the mainstream of this society. That is not true today. Public policy is now far removed from that concept, with schools routinely teaching immigrant children in their native language. In my view, language education in the United States today is potentially damaging to Latino immigrants and may in fact deny them the very opportunity that every other generation of immigrants has had in this country.

In California, for example, the Los Angeles Unified School District now has a bilingual education policy that requires students to stay in the program for a minimum of six years. A five-year-old Mexican immigrant child, or the child of immigrant parents, who comes into school in a heavily Latino area of Los Angeles will be put into a bilingual program at the age of five and will not get out of that program until he or she is eleven years old. By California law, those students have to receive at least twenty minutes of English instruction per day. The rest of their four-and-a-half-hour day, they are taught in Spanish. This would be bad enough if it were just happening to kids that come to school speaking Spanish, but a lot of five-year-olds in this program, particularly those born in the United States, have at least some knowledge of English when they enter school. Some of them have stronger English than they do Spanish, depending on where they live and whether or not they watch a lot of television or have a lot of English-speaking friends.

It turns out that even if kids come to school speaking English, they can be put in bilingual classes and taught in Spanish for most of the day. Children are placed in these programs as a result of something called the Home Language Survey, which is given to Latino parents, usually identified by surname. They are asked whether or not anyone in their home speaks a language other than English—not whether the child speaks it, not even whether the parents speak it, but whether *anyone* in the home speaks a language other than English. I grew up in New Mexico and my grandparents frequently spoke Spanish around me. Had I been a child going to school now, my parents would be required to check off the box indicating somebody spoke a language other than English. I did not speak any Spanish, but my grandparents did, and today I would be put into a Spanish bilingual class.

In fact, we are finding that there are a significant number of such English-speaking children being put into bilingual classes. Although it is difficult to get good statistics on this, we do know that nationally 60 percent of all the children in these programs are U.S.-born. These programs are costing educational agencies at least $5.5 billion annually. When we spend that kind of money on a policy that is trying to reinforce children's native language, we should not be surprised that it sometimes works and that some kids may in fact not learn English as rapidly as they could or should.

We have a variety of other policies related to ethnicity that I think may become barriers to the ultimate assimilation of all groups, particularly Latinos. We have affirmative action programs which assign benefits and preferences based on race or ethnicity. Immigrants are immediately eligible for such programs, even though they obviously have not suffered past discrimination in the United States. By definition, their children and grandchildren, as well as the children and grand-children of middle-class, successful, assimilated Hispanics, are also eligible for these programs.

I know this not just from research but from personal experience. When my oldest son graduated from high school in 1986, his grades were certainly not the exceptional kind that would normally net high-dollar offers of scholarships from around the country. Nonetheless, the scholarship offers poured in. One school offered him a twenty-five-thousand-dollar-a-year scholarship, and all he had to do to get it was apply. These letters came in unsolicited. He had not indicated any interest in going to these schools, but they were interested in him because of his ethnicity. Now, I am half Hispanic and my son is only one-quarter Hispanic. But the schools' only concern was that their "Hispanic" numbers look good. Needless to say, we turned them all down. My son went to a school where his grades and his SAT scores qualified him to attend on the basis of merit and not on the basis of ethnicity. When you give benefits on the basis of racial or ethnic ties, you are automatically reinforcing those ties. You are automatically giving people a reason to want to hold onto that ethnicity and define themselves in those terms. In fact, that is what we are doing across the board with affirmative action, and it is going to have an impact in terms of this immigration debate.

The vast majority of immigrants to the United States are eligible for these kinds of affirmative action set-asides. Asians tend not to benefit from these programs in universities because they already are doing quite well academically. In fact, some schools discriminate against Asians because they feel that Asians' academic achievement is giving them disproportionate representation. Asians do remain eligible for all the other set-aside programs, whether they are setting up a small business or buying a television station. This type of separate treatment by race reinforces racial and ethnic identity at the expense of assimilation.

We also have a very different kind of society than in the past with respect to our welfare policies. And I think this is what, in the final analysis, really motivated the vote in California. That vote for Proposition 187 was not just about immigrants. It was more precisely a vote about welfare policy. It allowed the voters of California to do something that voters no place else in the country could do—vote against welfare. I think there were a number of people who voted on that basis. The idea that people who were not legally entitled to be in the United States were being given welfare benefits outraged voters, despite the fact that working-age immigrants, both legal and illegal, are not high users of welfare. The two groups of foreign-born persons who are heavy users of welfare are refugees and elderly immigrants, many of whom have not worked long enough in this country to earn Social Security benefits for their retirement.

But even refugees are not taking advantage of the system. It is our federal refugee policy that dictates that refugees admitted through the refugee resettlement program are eligible to receive welfare. State welfare agencies have an incentive to keep those people on the books, so there are extraordinarily high welfare rates among Cambodians, Vietnamese, and Russian refugees, among others. Nonprofit, private, and religious agencies are far better suited to deal with refugees than government agencies. In fact, several test cases have shown these organizations to be successful in moving refugees off the welfare rolls much faster than government agencies do. What needs changing is the policy itself.

So what do we do about immigrants? Do we do what Pat Buchanan wants and erect a sort of Berlin Wall on our southern border? Do we engage in the kind of raids that we had in the United States in the 1930s, where people were rounded up and shipped back to Mexico? Some of those deported, by the way, were U.S. citizens, shipped to Mexico by accident. I do not think Americans want that. I think that kind of draconian effort is something that will be rejected by most Americans. But we do need to do something, and one of the things that I think we need to do is to get back to our notion of assimilation. Immigrants will only be accepted into society when we and they establish a kind of compact which says: You are welcome to come here, but we expect you to become part of our society. We expect you to learn the language. We expect you to adopt the traditions, morals, and values of the society. We expect you to become part of the civic community.

I believe that a lot of immigrants want that as well. But right now we have public policies that work against it. We have policies that teach children in their native language at the expense of English. We have policies in our social studies curriculum that fail to teach immigrant children about Thomas Jefferson and George Washington, the founders of this country, or fail to teach them to identify with the history of the United States as their nation. These policies fail to help them become Americans—so that they can celebrate Abraham Lincoln as a hero; so that they can feel good about the post–Civil War amendments that granted the right to vote, that granted equal protection of the laws, that ended slavery; so that they can feel that this history is also part of their own personal history. Until we begin to do this once more, we will have enclaves within our community that feel alienated.

Right now the trend in public education is very much against this. It is very much for multicultural education that reinforces ethnic and racial identity, that makes young people whose background is not English or European feel that they are different and that their identification should be with their ancestors. To me, this is a recipe for disaster. This is the undoing of our notion of nationhood, our notion that we are a nation made up of different people. In 1776 we adopted the national motto, *e pluribus unum*, "from many, one." That motto is essentially a rejection of the notion of multiculturalism and an affirmation that if we are to continue to welcome people to our shores, we must continue to think of ourselves as one nation and one people. I believe we must begin to aggressively promote this notion again. We need to do it in our schools and in our textbooks. Public policies should encourage and reinforce integration into the mainstream rather than encouraging people to remain separate, distinct, and outside the whole.

Notes

1. Statistics in this chapter are taken from Linda Chavez, *Out of the Barrio: Toward a New Politics of Hispanic Assimilation* (New York: Basic Books, 1991).

5

Politics of Cultural Wars

Heather R. Higgins

This chapter addresses the great philosophical divide which is splitting our country politically, often within the parties themselves. This philosophical divide is attributable to the dichotomy between relativism and natural law and the conflict between traditional and secular views.

You may have noticed lately how people, when they are engaging in political debate, often seem to be talking on entirely different tracks. That is because political debate at this point in time is not just about policies. It is in fact starting to be about the core principles which inform who we are and what we believe. Such rhetoric in the political sphere is unusual, because politicians, generally speaking, are lagging indicators. Politicians are not people to turn to for authoritative statements on principle. The Speaker of the House, Newt Gingrich, who is probably one of the single most interesting political figures out there now, has become an exception to this tendency. He frequently quotes from the Declaration of Independence, and he does it in a very entertaining way. He starts with the sentence "We hold these truths to be self-evident, that all men are created equal, that they are endowed by their Creator with certain unalienable Rights, that among these are Life, Liberty, and the Pursuit of Happiness. That, to secure these rights, Governments are instituted among Men, deriving their just powers from the consent of the governed." Then Congressman Gingrich does a send-up of the liberal alternative view. He points out that if liberals had written the Declaration, we would be holding that we are all just randomly gathered protoplasm who can for brief moments rationally conclude situationally ethically appropriate behaviors. It is amusing, but the point he is making is serious, and it gets to the core of what the divide is about.

That passage in the Declaration is quite clear about a number of things:

- One, it asserts that there is a truth. Which is something of a radical notion in this day of relativism.
- Two, it says that man was created by God, that we did not just randomly appear, that we are not just randomly gathered protoplasm.
- Three, it states that, in fact, there is a God, which can be a contended point.
- Four, it makes clear that the rights with which we are endowed came from our Creator, that rights did not just come out of the blue, that we do not make them up for ourselves, but that they actually come from someplace, that rights are external and unchanging.
- Finally, the passage is explicit in stating that government derives from the authority of the people. Government does not bestow rights. Rather, it guards those rights which attach to individuals and which preexist government, and it reflects the powers of the people.

Let me walk you through these premises and then show you how they are going to be reflected in the political debates, debates which you are starting to see happen, debates which are going to get, I predict, much more radical, much more quickly than most people appreciate. We have begun a seismic, paradigmatic shift, and such shifts happen very fast. For example, note the speed with which the consensus has evolved that affirmative action is a bad idea. Suddenly people are all willing to say it. People are ready to return to the truth we all know but have been reluctant to articulate, because the consequences of denying truth can be hideous and destructive.

Front Line broadcast a show called "Divided Memories."[1] It examined the fact that a lot of psychotherapists are focused on "recovering" memories. Certainly there are legitimate instances where the brain shuts out a too-hideous recollection. But what we are talking about here is, for example, "recovering" memories of child abuse after twenty or thirty years even where there is not only no evidence of child abuse, but affirmative evidence that there could not have been the described child abuse. There is, for example, the woman who has recovered the memory of the "fact" that she was stabbed in the stomach—in the first century B.C., in a previous life—and believes that is why she has a persistent stomachache. Or there is the woman who has recovered the fact that while still an ovum she got stuck in a fallopian tube on her way down to the uterus, which apparently accounts for why she has always been "stuck" in life.

Such monumental silliness would be amusing, save that this indoctrination has real consequences. There have been lawsuits lodged against fathers, for example, for alleged abuse, twenty years previous, of their daughters, despite the fact that in these cases there is absolutely no corroborating evidence of the charge and there is substantial evidence that such things never happened. Yet evidence or no evidence, the young woman has become absolutely convinced that this "truth," suggested over years of therapy, slowly remembered and fantastically embellished as therapy progresses, is in fact "true." A number of such therapists were asked on television how they knew whether these memories were true or not. Their response, uniformly, was that the question was irrelevant because there is no such thing as truth. In their view, whether you dream it, or whether you imagine it, or whether it actually happened is something to which they are *indifferent*. Since everybody has their own truth, reality and fantasy are equivalent. What matters to them is that you believe your truth to be true.

Relativism versus Natural Law

This idea, that there is no truth, is a function of the relativism which has so pervaded our culture in the last several decades. Relativism is an attitude which says that nothing is true except what you say is true. It is an attitude which expresses itself in the phrase "Don't impose your values on me." Relativism says all values are the same, that they are all equal. Which is, if you think about it, a silly idea. How can we ever be value-free? By definition, any "value-free" setting describes an accepted set of values. But beyond being silly, relativism leads to both personal and political problems. On the personal side, it produces an idea of liberty which is far removed from the idea of liberty with which this country was founded. It is an idea of liberty that says: Go ahead and make it up as you go along. All the choices you make are equal in life. Who are we to judge what you decide to do? Essentially, this conception of liberty confuses liberty with license, and contrasts poorly with the idea of authentic liberty. Authentic liberty is necessary to human dignity; it is the liberty to do what you ought to do, not the license to do whatever you want to do. It rests on the premise that people in fact have a higher end, and that striving for that end is the source of our dignity.

Relativism also has problems on the political level, because if a relativist seeks to know the good, his criterion must ultimately be utility. For a utilitarian, there are no limits to government power because there can always be an important enough end to justify removing limits. Further, the relativist has no moral ground for criticizing, for example, Nazi Germany. You'll remember that the Nuremberg trials were not possible without natural law, without the idea that there was in fact some universal truth to which we should all be held accountable. According to relativism, there was nothing "wrong" with what the Nazis did. The relativist, if he is honest, will hold that moral condemnation of the Nazis is just a reflection of a worldview no more valid than any other; the Nazis' values were as legitimate for them as your values are for you.

Yet as Lincoln said in one of his debates with Stephen Douglas, "there is no right to do wrong." Now, where does this understanding of truth, to which Lincoln referred and which most of us share, and which is so different from the relativist view, come from? How do we justify it? And why do we believe it? Look again to the second and third points in that statement from the Declaration: the idea that we are created by God and that there is a God.

Traditional versus Secular Views

Here is the heart of the division between the traditional and the secular views of the nature of man. The traditional view, which probably most of you hold, is that people are capable of good and bad, and that while they may be influenced by these factors, ultimately they have a choice as to how they choose to behave. What is good is not arbitrary, but is determined by God, or natural law. In contrast, the secular view holds that men are themselves good, and thus are themselves the authors of what constitutes the good. As a result, each man himself is the arbiter of what is true, what is not true, and what values are good. It is a view which also requires, since we are good, that evil be external to us, the function of outside social forces. If you commit a crime, you couldn't help it because you were poor, you were discriminated against, you were abused by your parents. You even hear people argue that if someone is shot, the gun did it; if a country is a threat, it is the fault of nuclear weapons. Blame is attached to an external force, rarely to the specific behavior of individuals.

Such thinking leads to a couple of different ideas which we find pervasive in society. One is the replacement of the concept of the responsible individual with the idea of the group. We are all members of groups; those groups are defined by the external social forces to which we are subject. Thus, it is not a question of free will affecting your behavior, but of those external social forces which afflict you and your group. The holy trinity of such determinism is, of course, race, gender, and class. This in turn leads to the idea of people as victims. I am sure you all have heard of the term "the politics of victimization." It is perhaps most evident in court trials where it is used to subvert traditional notions of justice, which hold individuals accountable for their behaviors. In, for example, the Menendez case, responsibility for behavior was obviated by an alleged pathology, real or not. Or, on the *Front Line* show, you had people saying that they were in therapy, checking for recovered memories which would explain why they were not as happy as they thought they ought to be; in so doing, they were essentially seeking the status of victim of a past incident as a way of exonerating themselves from responsibility for their current unhappiness. In some sense, that is much easier than having to be responsible for pursuing one's own happiness. Remember, the Declaration does not say that we have a right to be happy; it says that we have a right to pursue happiness. If anything, we have an obligation to pursue happiness, but there are no guarantees. The traditional worldview does not assume that happiness is a natural state. Yet the logic of the secular view asserts that absent those external social forces, we would necessarily be happy. Thus, the great cop-out to victimhood.

Still another consequence of the secular worldview is that if you believe that people are victims of external social forces, then you redefine what is compassion and what is justice. Justice, traditionally, is always the core public virtue for any functioning society, because the precondition for people cohering as a society is that everyone knows the rules, and everyone knows that they are all going to be judged more or less objectively by those rules. Justice requires that individuals be accountable for their behavior. Instead, we've replaced that with an exculpatory compassion. This is understandable enough if you feel that people are victims of external social forces. Then, in fact, the logical response is first to feel sorry for the victims and excuse their behavior, and second to demonstrate that you care by showing sufficient will to address those external social forces.

Compassion

As David Horowitz has pointed out, the right thinks that a lot of people on the left are misguided and stupid, while assorted people on the left describe people on the right as not just stupid, but evil. The reason that the left so vilifies people on the right is precisely that the secular viewpoint leads one to believe in the concept of will, the concept that we can perfect society, and thus that we can perfect man, through sufficient will applied against pernicious social forces. In this view, anyone who doesn't go along with this program of the exercise of sufficient will is, by definition, condemning the rest of us to an imperfect life in a world of evil social forces. This question of will becomes, in itself, the measure of morality. The measure of morality is the purity of your intentions. In the politics of intentions, for example, the amount of money you are willing to spend on the poor lets us gauge whether in fact you actually care about the poor, even if spending that money is in reality counterproductive to their well-being. "Compassion" thus defined requires refraining from judgment of the individual who is the object of your attentions. Such an approach is, in fact, antithetical to the much more intellectually serious moral tradition that says that in order to demonstrate compassion you first have to define what is good, and then assist someone to receive it or to attain it. That is at the core, to a great part, of much of what is going on in the welfare debate. It is not how much money you spend, it is whether you treat people as creatures of God, as spiritual beings with more than material needs, as human beings whose behavior ultimately affects their life outcomes. Or whether you just feed their dysfunction and let them continue to be dependent.

Another subversion of the idea of compassion derives from its misguided institutionalization. Compassion traditionally is an individual virtue, applied necessarily person-to-person as a reciprocal act (as opposed to justice, which is, again, a public virtue and necessary to the effective functioning of the state). By having compassion applied selectively by the state, you ultimately subvert a sense of justice. For example, affirmative action preferences and set asides, however well intended, end up not only hurting the intended beneficiaries but ultimately subverting the idea that the rules are fair, that the playing field is level.

Rights and Moral Obligations

We have created a fictitious "right" to compassion, a new entitlement to government-provided compassion, and here too we see the effect of the secular viewpoint, wherein we can make up rights as we go along. Look again at the

Declaration. Rights are endowed by God. Rights are always the lowest form of social obligation, not the highest, which allowed Jefferson to call on all men to recognize them. Rights, traditionally understood, have certain defining characteristics, which derive from the idea that rights come from somewhere, namely, natural law or God:

- First, rights preexist us; they preexist government. They do not get made up by a government whenever convenient (for example, a "right" to health care) or dropped whenever inconvenient (the rights to life and liberty for Jews in Nazi Germany).

- Second, rights are negative, in that they require nothing from anyone else. Thus, the right to liberty, or the right to pursue happiness, requires no obligation on your part to cause me to achieve these things, only that you let me alone to try to achieve these things.

- Third, rights are universal, applying simultaneously to everyone at all times. If a "right" requires that for some people to receive other people must be taken from, that is not a right.

- Fourth, because we are not atomistic individuals but human beings who live in communities, rights carry corollary obligations, which is something that we too conveniently forget.

In the political realm, what we need to understand is that the shift is going to be away from the language of rights, which is limited and inappropriate, to the language of moral obligation, a much higher calling. Moral obligation, deriving as it does from an understanding of human beings as creatures of God with a spiritual capacity for good, implies that in a free society the idea of exercising compassion, not as a forced government entitlement program, but through voluntary association, is necessary to our development of ourselves as civic beings, as citizens. Government, again as is said in the Declaration, is derived from the authority of the people. Government is not something that imposes itself on the people except through their will. The people are the government, and the idea that you see going on now in the political discourse is that of returning government to the people. The fancy word for this is subsidiarity.[2] Block grants, for example, are a step closer to the ultimate goal of turning over to private associations and local communities what is best done at those levels.

Applications to Current Political Issues

How do the principles I have outlined play out in some of the political issues facing us? If you look at the balanced budget fight, which is over having a balanced budget amendment and is over the budget itself, as well as the unfunded mandate fight, these issues are not just about dollars. They are about the principle that we are responsible, as citizens, for what our government does, and for its future. They are about the principle that we have an obligation to pay for ourselves, not to foist the burdens of ourselves on future generations, and that we therefore have a moral obligation to exercise fiscal restraint and live within our means.

The Shays law, which was the first act passed by Congress in 1995, says that the government should be accountable to the people, that it is not above the people, that it is the servant of the people, and that its servants must be held accountable to the same laws which the people themselves are held to.

The idea of block grants, as mentioned above, is the idea of returning the power home. It is an expression of the idea that we should take power out of the hands of government and return it to local communities and to private voluntary associations.

The welfare debate, which is going to get very hard shortly, is about treating human beings as creatures of God, as opposed to treating them as animals who have no needs other than to be housed and fed. It is about understanding that compassion, to be effectively administered, needs to be done on a one-to-one basis, not through some bureaucratic agency that is filling out a form and writing out a check.

The affirmative action debate rests on the premise that all people are equal before the law, and that as such a cardinal rule of any society that is going to remain unified is that we must all treat each other equally, applying the same rules to everyone. It is an aspiration that was expressed by Martin Luther King Jr. in his statement that we should be a color-blind society where people are not "judged by the color of their skin but by the content of their character,"[3] and it is a refutation of the idea that we are merely members of groups, not individuals.

These are only some of the issues that will continue to come before us. It is important to understand that even though not all the politicians get this yet (and they still don't get a lot of things), much of this debate is going to be conducted on the moral plane of first principles. It is a debate that we as a nation have too long done without, and that we as a people should welcome.

Notes

1. *Front Line*, "Divided Memories," broadcast by PBS, April 4, 1995.

2. Pope Pius XI first formulated this concept in *Quadragesimo Anno*; in so doing, he drew on and reformulated some of the ideas in Aristotle and Aquinas with a Christian Augustinian overlay, as well as the ideas of Wilhelm Emmanuel von Ketteler, Bishop of Mainz. See entries by Robert Royal on "Subsidiarity" and "Catholic Social Doctrine" in the forthcoming *Catholic Encyclopedia*, as well as Thomas C. Kohler, *Quadragesimo Anno (1931), A Century of Catholic Social Thought*, ed. George Weigel and Robert Royal (Washington, D.C.: Ethics and Public Policy Center, 1991), Chapter 2, pp. 27–43.

3. Martin Luther King Jr., "I Have a Dream," in *Testament of Hope: the Essential Writings of Martin Luther King Jr.*, ed. James Melvin Washington, (San Francisco: Harper and Row Publishers, 1986), Chapter 36, 219.

6

Who Killed Dr. Kildare?

Midge Decter

Popular culture is a very tricky subject to get hold of—particularly the popular culture of one's own time, and most particularly if one's own time is an era of advanced technology (simply because there is so much more of it). One of the main difficulties connected with talking about, say, the movies or television is the problem of how, as Yeats would say, to tell the dancer from the dance, that is, how to tell if a certain product of popular culture is merely the expression of, or is itself the creator of, certain responses and attitudes.

This particular difficulty in connection with American popular culture came to be exacerbated in the period immediately following World War II, when movies, pulp fiction, comic books, and so on came for the first time to be the objects of serious academic study. This brought the whole enterprise to a new level of self-consciousness, so that, for instance, movie rating could become "film criticism," honored men of letters could write about comic strips, and, as we witnessed particularly in the 1960s, people could even begin to manufacture folk songs.

Now, there may have been a deep psychosocial reason for this curious new display of national/cultural self-consciousness—but that there was in fact such a reason, or what it might have been, would be hard to say. It does somehow seem worth mentioning the ironic detail that, at least to begin with, among the main practitioners of this new academic discipline were a number of refugee German scholars, who were no doubt grateful for the sanctuary America had offered them but whose responses to American culture generally were, to say the least, far from admiring.

In the early days of the discipline, of course, the term "popular culture" was used to refer primarily to the movies—radio, except for a handful of soap operas, having somehow escaped the Teutonic scrutiny, as for the most part had popular novels and mass magazines The movies were certainly no more ubiquitous than print and radio, but they had come for a number of reasons—the most obvious of these being that they were the one medium of communication shared universally and simultaneously by Americans of all circumstances and regions of the country—to be seen as the primary makers and/or reflections of American myths. (And how the academics and critics in those early postwar days loved to dig for the mythical! I remember reading in the literary quarterlies of the early 1950s more than one or two essays about *Moby Dick*—which was all the rage back then—that went on for ten thousand words or so without mentioning that the book had something to do with a whale. The high literary life notwithstanding, it would, I think, just possibly be true to say that some part of the search for the great American myth had to do with the way it afforded certain high- and serious-minded people a high- and serious-minded reason for subjecting themselves to the effortless thrills and easy pleasures that popular culture was so plentifully supplying to their fun-seeking, low-minded countrymen.)

Be all that as it may, when it came to both power and ubiquity, the movies for obvious reasons were by the end of the 1950s to prove a mere shadow, a fleeting flicker in the dark, as compared with television. Indeed, so overwhelming a force has television become in American daily life—I don't need to bore you with the statistics; everybody beyond the age of ten has heard them by now—that analysts of American culture have just about given up the effort to get some kind of analytic handle on it.

Except, that is, for the making of certain simple, flat-out moral judgments. Almost from the first moment that television became a mass commodity we have been treated to a series of stern indictments of the medium: Television, some say, is responsible for the failure of our educational system, making children into the mere passive recipients of instant entertainment and smothering their capacity to read and learn for themselves. Or, say others, television is a major contributor to juvenile violence, for by the time a child has reached puberty, he has witnessed the dramatization of upwards of ten thousand—or is it twenty thousand? or maybe two hundred thousand—murders. Or, still others charge, television has had a deadening effect on family life, having replaced real conversation. Or it has debased even further a deplorable standard of taste. Or it has undermined individuality, or, or, or . . . take your pick of one or more, or all.

And just as many of the people who first elevated the analysis—actually psychoanalysis—of American mass culture to the status of an academic discipline were actually foreign to this culture, many, if not most, of the people who launch these moral attacks on the power of television are the kind of people who seldom watch television themselves—except maybe for public service broadcasting—and thus do not in fact know the half of it.

They also, in my opinion, get it wrong. Indeed, what is commonly said in disparagement of television is in some sense more intellectually crude and philistine than the programming it is complaining against. Take the complaint that television retards children in learning to read. It is true that children in the age of television are in constant need of external stimulation, and that television has much, if not everything, to do with this. However, what has actually put the crimp in reading is the fact that children are not being properly taught or seriously required to read in school; television has turned out to be a most convenient alibi for, among other things, half a century of disastrous educational doctrine. Children who have been taught to be genuinely comfortable with reading (most of whom, I would be willing to bet, have basically been taught at home) read *and* watch television. Sometimes, as was the case with my own youngest child and is now the case with my oldest grandchild, they do both at the same time. (You might think this is impossible. I certainly did lo those many years ago, when I nagged and nagged, but be assured that both of these people are, for their respective ages, highly literate.) In other words, the problem of television and the problem of literacy are both far more complex.

As for deadening family conversation, so many of the people who nowadays—to be sure, with perfect justice—deplore the condition of the family and proclaim the need to revitalize this essential institution seem, in the great solemnity of their intention, to have forgotten what the actual daily texture of family relations is. Family conversation? Question: Well, Joey, did you have a good time in school today? Answer: Yeah. Question: What did you do? Answer: Nothing. That colloquy is in its way undoubtedly important for both children and parents—at least, most of them who are in the position to do so go through it on every appropriate occasion—but as actual conversation it is strictly symbolic.

Or take my own favorite stricture, the one about the contribution of television to juvenile crime. Talk about providing an alibi for someone's or something else's failure! Anyone who has ever paid genuine attention to children knows how bloodthirsty they are, especially, though certainly not exclusively—God forgive me for mentioning it—little boys. The point is that as in the case of fairy tales—which are no longer part of the canon of childhood for enlightened parents because they are too grisly (and no doubt because their language is too difficult)—the action and mayhem and killing on television and in the movies serve children's natural taste for blood precisely by being *proxies* for it. Violent juveniles are not imitating television; they are doing something entirely different—if only we had the spiritual genius to get to the bottom of it. Surely at least part of what they are doing is expressing their need and longing for at least some simulacrum of manliness. In any case, not all the shootings on television put together can explain a fifteen-year-old's pulling a gun or a knife on a classmate over the possession of a jacket or a group of twelve- and thirteen-year-olds' setting fire to an old wino sleeping on a park bench. To correlate the increase in juvenile crime with an increase in the number of hours of television being watched each week, as a number of highly respected social critics in our midst are wont to do, is, I am afraid, to put the cart oh so conveniently before the horse.

There is no doubt that we Americans have become inured to violence to a deplorable degree. That, however, is in my opinion because so much of our public thinking and speech over the past thirty years has been devoted to alibiing violence, whether in behalf of the poor, the black, the addicted, or the insane. Find enough justifying causes for violence, and you begin to domesticate the idea, give it house-room. It may well be that the producers of television and the movies keep raising the ante on bloodshed precisely in answer to the raised dramatic demands that follow from our having forgiven so much.

But, you might ask, if I claim that the moralizing criticisms of television are mostly invalid, why do I say that the critics of television don't know the half of how truly problematic it has become? Because there is a serious problem with this medium, but the problem is a different one from that which its critics have been harping on. It is, in fact, that television, far from being a wasteland, has become much too good. What I am referring to here is not public-affairs television—which with few exceptions *is* a wasteland—but precisely major-network entertainment. And what I mean by much too good is much too accomplished, too well produced, too well written and well directed; in short, too effectively entertaining in a genuinely dreadful way.

Let me explain with the following example. Back in the early 1960s, there was a series about a young doctor named Kildare, played by Richard Chamberlain, and his mentor, Dr. Gillespie, played, if memory serves, by Raymond Massey. This series was based on a novel, which had earlier been made into a movie, starring—for the benefit of those still interested in ancient history—Lew Ayres as Dr. Kildare and Lionel Barrymore as Dr. Gillespie. There was in the days of Drs. Kildare and Gillespie a convention that governed television hospitals, and also at least some television police precincts: the hero of the show was to be a young practitioner who in moments of crisis (which would arrive reliably, one crisis to an episode) would be admonished by his wise and case-hardened elder to get control of his tender, quivering empathy for some patient (or in the case of cops, some victim), pull up his socks, and get on with the work of fulfilling his professional responsibility. Dr. Kildare worked full time in a hospital—was a resident, perhaps, though I cannot remember that any reference was made to his status; he certainly practiced full-scale medicine, he certainly practiced it on his own, and he was certainly fully responsible for many a wonderful, if not, indeed, miraculous, cure. And he did all this selflessly, untiringly, and with great sweetness of temperament. Moreover, Dr. Kildare had no private life: no wife, no children, no girlfriend, no personal history of any kind. The drama of this series was the drama of Dr. Kildare's patients only, and of his interaction with them. If now and then there was the suggestion that a potentially romantic spark had been ignited between him and some brave and suffering—and, of course, beautiful—young patient being attended by him, she was clearly doomed either to be returned to the arms of a suddenly materializing husband or to die.

Not too many years later there was another television doctor named Ben Casey—as I remember it, even more popular than Dr. Kildare—whose weekly series hewed to the same convention, except that it was neither so saccharine nor quite so predictable, and not quite so dreadfully badly written. Nor was Casey handsome as Kildare was. He was dour and rather taciturn—that was, as they say in showbiz, his shtick—which provided, on the one hand, more drama and, on the other, more verisimilitude. I don't mean to exaggerate: verisimilitude about doctors or medicine or hospitals, or for that matter about life itself, was no part of the deal being made between screen and audience in either of these shows.

But *elevation* was. The very point about these heroes, especially young Dr. Kildare, was that they were precisely not what serious drama or literature would have required them to be, not complex but simple, not full of ambivalence but innocent of heart; and their weaknesses—never given into but always, always overcome—were the weaknesses that attend simplicity of nature and innocence of heart. To see reruns of one of these programs today[1] is to marvel at the degree of their high- and simple-mindedness. But it was exactly for that quality that millions continued to be entranced by them for long years.

Compare today's equivalent hospital drama, at this writing the program with the highest Nielsen ratings on all of television: *ER* (which stands, of course, for Emergency Room). *ER* is a series about a group of residents who staff the emergency room of an urban hospital. The convention that governs this series (as well as one on a different network called *Chicago Hope* that began as, and at least so far has failed to become, *ER*'s main competitor) is that each episode is studded with the misadventures and consequent medical needs of a group of patients who are brought into the emergency room in the course of a single shift (whether day or night is not always clear). There is, to be sure, a more or less leading character among the group, but all are in full view and engagement each week.[2] The most important relations in the show are not between doctors and patients but among the doctors, who are, by the way, all clearly designated as residents; a senior practitioner shows up only now and then, usually either to chastise or to offer grudging approval of some emergency procedure. Moreover, the audience is kept apprised of all their extra medical private difficulties: one has a wife who wants to pursue her own career in a different city; one is a philanderer who has driven the nurse he truly loves into the arms (and bed) of a colleague; one is a woman who is touchy about whether she is receiving the proper measure of respect; one is a black who is desperate to become an attending physician and perpetually angry about his own desperation. All, of course, are first-rate doctors—here the convention remains fixed; otherwise how could we bear to watch them working?—who work like demons and sometimes perform medical prodigies. The dramatic quality of this show depends very much on its pace, which is, to put it mildly, frenetic. Ambulances arrive to deliver up new emergencies, as it seems, every two minutes. At least once in every episode, virtually the entire cast is engaged in rushing someone severely damaged from ambulance to gurney to operating room, stopping along the way only to hook the patient to various I.V.'s and to get his failed heart beating again by the application of electric shocks, meanwhile rushing about and issuing orders to one another; and in between the audience is invited to attend to a variety of other emergency cases involving such patients as hallucinators, Alzheimer's sufferers, children whose bones have been broken by abuse, and homeless winos. These dramas, large and small, are extremely well acted and usually very well paced, the personal and the medical being balanced in a proportion that generally keeps the frenzy from being merely wearying. All this notwithstanding, *ER* is utterly preposterous—far, far more unreal, for all its social candor, than *Dr. Kildare* ever was. For one thing, anyone who has ever had the pleasure of being in a hospital emergency room knows that it is a place whose most characteristic component is a large waiting room presided over by a certain number of bureaucratic record keepers and full of long-suffering people, in both senses of the term, who are waiting to get through a door on the other side of which they will be attended to by doctors and nurses who may be good at what they do but are anything but in a frenzied hurry. Even more preposterous is the idea that an emergency-room resident would himself rush a dying patient upstairs to an operating room and, knowing there was no time to lose but unable to scare up a licensed neurosurgeon, perform the indicated brain surgery himself. Here again, however, it is not verisimilitude that is supposed to be on offer, but something else: psychological adventure, which is today's sophisticated and highly reductive replacement for heroism. It is crucial for the protagonists of such adventure that they be at least very good and preferably brilliant at what they do—viz., the doctors of *Chicago Hope* as well as those of *ER* and a whole array of policemen, public defenders, prosecutors, and most especially detectives—and at the same time beset with difficulty, anguish, loneliness, crises of conscience toward their families and now and then toward their work, sometimes alcoholism, and hopefully even, way back when, a police record.

Psychological adventure certainly makes for a higher level of dramatic invention than does old-fashioned heroism and by the same token may seem to a viewer, at least momentarily, to be more "real," more "truthful." Its underlying intention, however—and ultimately its lasting effect—is to reduce everything to ordinary size: drama for an audience that as ever is seeking instant heroes but at the same time is too knowing to take its heroism at face value. The characters whose fortunes audiences seem now to be most engaged by are people behind whose exploits lurk the kinds of predicaments that are aired on the afternoon talk shows.

Nor is this sophistication confined to the so-called dramatic series: sit-coms, too, are for the most part no longer funny by virtue of their clowning or silliness but have been turning ever more worldly and clever. Even the youngest characters in them—should they, for example, be only five or six years old—must be wisecrackers, their very place in the comedy depending on the disjuncture between their size and their sophistication. Even they, for instance, could not be shown to be watching *Dr. Kildare* without making witty comment on it. And then there is the cartoon for grown-ups, *The Simpsons,* watched avidly by a massive audience and now going on and on in reruns. The hero of this show is a preadolescent boy, the first-born of a family that includes a genius younger sister and a baby, a boy whose father is a drunk and whose daily life seems to consist of a variety of tactics for living at odds with a world all of whose inhabitants have a low and unloving opinion of him. He might be today's clowning avatar of Charlie Chaplin's tramp; he could certainly, with only a slight shift of perspective, break your heart; but far from being comedy in the Chaplin sense, *The Simpsons* is a witty sneer, both at its eponymous family and at life. The show can in fact be quite brilliantly funny, but the laughter it evokes is the laughter of the abyss.

It is in this sense that television, the great reducer, the great squasher of high hearts and innocence, is a depressing cultural voice. To be sure, what it tells us is not simply its own invention; such a vast grinding machine of talent would simply not have room or time for an original social idea. But what it tells us is being ever more entertainingly, and thus ever more seductively, put.

There was once an idea—indeed, businessmen seem to be ever more actively exploring it—that cable broadcasting would break the power of the major networks. Perhaps it will. Perhaps this change will bring a whole new era to public entertainment and popular culture. But from where I sit, which is in the presence of some seventy television channels, it is hard to believe that so much scruffiness, amateurism, tiresome chitchat, revolting self-exposure, and just plain smut as cable television now provides would prove in any sense a happy substitute for, or will in fact replace the audience for, network entertainment.

So what are we to do about the power of television over the life of this country? The answer is, I don't know. I am certain that it is not useful to hold television responsible for problems for which it is not in fact responsible. The change, if change there be, must, I am afraid, start with *us.* Change men's minds and hearts, if I may borrow a familiar slogan, and those whose business it is to profit from them will follow.

Before concluding, I must add a footnote about two other forms of television. Omitting comment on the porn, both homosexual and heterosexual, which is to be seen, at least where I live, on two separate cable channels late in the evening—basically this is intended to serve as advertisements for escort services and thus belongs more to the world of commerce than to the world of entertainment—the two forms of television I am talking about are MTV and the talk shows, this latter involving various forms of self-display on the part of people who find themselves, to put it mildly, in strange circumstances. Two ladies who have been made pregnant by the same man and wish to involve both the studio audience and the viewing public in their vendetta with the gentleman in question in full view would provide a good example of the kind of fare to be found on these shows, which are, one reads in the papers, overtaking soap operas in popularity. My own favorite was a company of ladies who appeared on the Oprah Winfrey show, a couple of years ago, under the rubric of "women who marry their rapists."

These shows have merely replaced the old circus freak shows featuring such figures as the six-hundred-pound baby and Jo-Jo the dog-faced boy. They are neither skilled nor unskilled, such talk shows, depending not on their production values but on their power to shock and repel. In my opinion, though they are popular now, these shows do not have much of a future, for repulsion is a response that wears rather thin after a while. And while some have overtaken soap operas, others are being canceled for lack of an audience. Mostly they bear witness to how far in self-exposure people are willing to go in order to be on television.

MTV, the other of the two forms of television I referred to, on the other hand, has become a genuinely powerful new popular art form. The thing one must understand about MTV is that it is on the whole visually very brilliant. Extremely stylish and inventive, MTV is a stroke of genius on the part of the music industry, for it is doubtful that without those visual aids, the young on whom the industry has come so much to depend would be able to distinguish one song or one performer from another. This new form seems to be a direct outgrowth of that period of television whose highest creativity and savvy were to be found not in the programming but in the commercials. In any case, it too tends, like most successful sit-coms and dramatic series, to be both frenetic and sophisticated, in the saddest of all possible meanings of that term. Tipper Gore's campaign against some of this stuff is honorable, but in my opinion misguided. For it is not so much the *minds* of the kids that are at stake here but their nervous systems, and with them, the kids' sense of the pace of life from *Mister Rogers' Neighborhood*, so to speak, to Michael Jackson and beyond.

Again, what to do about it? Whatever the answer, it is one that lies far beyond the purview of television itself, and far, far beyond the reach of mere policy.

Notes

1. *Ben Casey* is occasionally rerun on one of the more obscure cable channels, but so far, it would seem, at least to New Yorkers, that his colleague Dr. Kildare has been left to gather dust in some broadcasting museum.

2. Not surprisingly, just as the conventions that governed *Kildare* and *Casey* also applied to more than a few cops, so the far more dramatically complex and gripping *ER* convention according to which it is the group as a whole which functions as the hero applies as well to the most popular of today's police precincts, namely, that featured in a show called *NYPD Blue*.

7

The Restoration of Citizenship and Civic Culture

Robert Royal

Let us begin by putting things in historical perspective. In many ways, we are all enjoying levels of prosperity and political liberties that would be the envy of virtually all peoples at all times in the history of the human race. Though we allow ourselves a lot of casual grumbling about fluctuations in economic growth and worry about some troubling signs of decline in various sectors of the society, even Americans from earlier generations would largely be glad to trade places with us today. We face no major foreign threats, and the basic tranquillity of our domestic affairs continues to make America a haven and a magnet for immigrants from all parts of the globe. All this and more can be said on the positive side of the ledger at present. And anyone who still wants to denounce the evils of capitalism and the dangers of the consumer society must first acknowledge, as even Karl Marx once did, the unprecedented achievements of modern markets and democracies.[1]

But to focus on our economic and political achievements alone, or primarily, it seems to me, is a mistake that lands us into the same materialist evaluation that made Marxism false and pernicious. I do not believe that any of these material factors is a very reliable guide to the state of our civic culture. In fact, I would like to emphasize at the outset that the great emphasis we place on political and economic questions, and on politics and economics as a solution to our current situation, may itself be a historical aberration. Historically, most societies have recognized that, yes, their health and welfare rest on good public institutions, but depend even more on the character and virtues of their peoples. Virtuous peoples around the world may have been repressed and corrupted by bad institutions, but even good institutions, as I believe we are beginning to recognize in this country, cannot entirely make up for—and may even be threatened by—social decay.

For example, several credible sources in our Western tradition warn us that there are dangers, as well as benefits, in wealth. Even secular views like the old civic humanist tradition feared that humanity was doomed to an endless cycle of: virtuous effort leading to prosperity; decadence owing to ease; and renewed virtue in the face of challenges springing from decadence. Figures as diverse as Polybius, Machiavelli, and Gibbon saw this cycle as a virtual historical law. Human nature, they thought, was simply too weak to remain virtuous in conditions of peace and affluence. The Scriptures, too, contain many warnings about the false attractions of wealth and add (in the Jerusalem Bible's graphic version): "Man in his prosperity forfeits intelligence: he is one with the cattle doomed to slaughter" (Psalms 49:19–20). Neither the old humanists nor the psalmist ever studied social science at a modern university, but perhaps they had noticed something all the same.

The specific danger of modern wealth is twofold, it seems to me. On the one hand, the wealthy, like the wealthy in all times and places, may be unjust and indifferent to the less fortunate. On the other hand, even our poor in modern societies are so well off materially by historical standards that the connections between bad behavior and its unpleasant consequences have become weakened to the point of no longer being easily even believed. I don't think only welfare has had a demoralizing influence on the poor, as everyone, liberal and conservative, now admits. Our general prosperity, too, coupled with decay in social standards have made, say, illegitimacy or drug use less "inconvenient," in Doug Besharov's phrase, than ever before in the past.[2]

Our situation, however, is not without precedent. In fact, there are two or three phases in our history that we might look at more carefully for suggestions and encouragement as to how to deal with our current problems. In the earlier years of the American republic, for example, the upsurge in popular economic and political activity seemed to many of the best minds, including some of the surviving Founding Fathers, to portend disaster. Everything seemed chaotic. People were moving west and disrupting family and other social ties. Religion as a binding force was on the decline. By 1813, John Adams asked: "When? Where? and How? is the present Chaos to be arranged in order?"[3]

The answer was, broadly, popular religion. As Nathan Hatch traces brilliantly in his *The Democratization of American Christianity* (Yale University Press), it was largely thanks to Methodists that moral regeneration and a renewal of social order occurred. The circuit riders went out into the new lands and among the sectors of society who had left the old, more hierarchical European Protestant denominations. In so doing, they became perhaps the single most powerful force in keeping the country together up until the Civil War.

Another case closer to our own time and more similar to our own situation arose toward the end of the nineteenth century. Historical comparisons are never, of course, entirely exact, but according to James Q. Wilson, both England and

America at the time faced some difficulties with which we are quite familiar: industrialization, urbanization, immigration, and simultaneous poverty and affluence. Elites, both secular and religious, reacted, says Wilson, "by asserting an ethics of self-control, whereas in the late twentieth century they reacted to many of the same forces by asserting an ethos of self-expression."[4]

Another recent example is telling. In July 1994, we celebrated the anniversary of the liberation of Paris—one of the truly heroic moments in a just struggle against a singularly evil regime. The America of the 1940s had just come through a very hard decade, economically and socially, in the Depression, and, contrary to what our current social science wisdom might tell us, actually experienced reduced crime rates and greater family cohesiveness.[5] We are so used to mechanical analysis of conditions today that we almost entirely overlook the importance of the attitudes people bring to hardship. Some grow stronger and emerge from trial even more ready to sacrifice for the good. The seventy-year-old veterans who reenacted their parachute jumps over Normandy during the summer belong to a generation whose like we shall not see again for some time.

By contrast, we also recently celebrated, if that is the right term, the twenty-fifth anniversary of Woodstock. I was at Woodstock and mostly remember it as loud, muddy, and unpleasant. Woodstock and its ethos have been often criticized, and it is so easy to do that I would not want to join entirely in the trashing of the sixties culture—almost entirely, but not entirely. While many forms of self-indulgence became socially acceptable in the sixties and seventies, those decades did also open society up to a far greater acceptance of American blacks, of women, of greater social justice in general. Not all the ways these social openings occurred were altogether positive, but let us be grateful that the country went through some wrenching experiences, including Vietnam, with as little damage as it did.

The legacy of Woodstock as greater freedom to do your own thing, however, has left the society, especially the most vulnerable parts of the society, less well off than ever. The sexual revolution and the social upheavals of the past couple of decades have harmed the black family, for example, more than did slavery and racism, to judge from the statistics on illegitimacy and family breakup. And this during the time that opportunities were opening and economic advances made as never before in black America.

Perhaps this portrait of the two halves of society I have painted seems insensitive or uncaring, so I would like to spell out what I mean further. It is almost impossible to attend any discussion without someone quoting Alexis de Tocqueville, who has become the poster boy for all efforts, of whatever stripe, to analyze our current situation. Tocqueville is often quoted now for his warning near the end of *Democracy in America* about the kind of soft despotism that threatens nations of our sort, and I suppose it's worthwhile to quote him yet another time. Tocqueville warned of what happens to citizens wholly occupied in the pursuit of "petty and paltry" pleasures:[6]

> Each of them living apart, is as a stranger to the fate of all the rest; his children and his private friends constitute to him the whole of mankind. As for the rest of his fellow citizens, he is close to them, but does not see them; he touches them, but he does not feel them; he exists only in himself and for himself alone; and if his kindred still remain to him, he may be said at any rate to have lost his country.

Tocqueville goes on to warn about how governments then come to be seen:

> Above this race of men stands an immense and tutelary power, which takes upon itself alone to secure their gratifications and to watch over their fate. That power is absolute, minute, regular, provident, and mild.... For their happiness such a government willingly labors, but it chooses to be the sole agent and the only arbiter of that happiness; it provides for their security, foresees and supplies their necessities, facilitates their pleasures, manages their principal concerns, directs their industry, regulates the descent of property, and subdivides their inheritances: what remains, but to spare them all the care of thinking, and the trouble of living?

Sound familiar? How about this?

> After having thus successively taken each member of the community in its powerful grasp and fashioned him at will, the supreme power then extends its arm over the whole community. It covers the surface of society with a network of small complicated rules, minute and uniform, through which the most original minds and the most energetic characters cannot penetrate, to rise above the crowd. The will of man is not shattered, but softened, bent, and guided; men are seldom forced by it to act, but they are constantly restrained from acting.

For me and for many people, I suspect, this is a powerfully prescient portrait of the kind of society in which we now find ourselves: prosperous, tolerant, individualized in a strange sort of malaise—a term that oddly keeps recurring in discussions as if we were, for all our wealth and successes, a stagnating society.

Yet I would like to propose that we look to a different, and less-studied, text by Tocqueville for our future deliberations. In his *Memoir on Pauperism*, Tocqueville speculates on why it is that in the nineteenth century the poor in Britain, who enjoyed levels of wealth twelve times the level of the poor in Portugal (then Europe's least-developed country), were far more demoralized than their Portuguese counterparts. He coins the phrase "the condition of the poor" to try to get at a whole tangle of factors, over and above material welfare, that enable us to judge whether being poor has passed over into a kind of moral destitution, or whether it is a livable human condition.

I think such a concept has great relevance to our own reflections on "the poor." The rural poor in America are most overlooked because they form such a small part of the overall poverty population. But it might be interesting if some social scientist were to study whether the "condition," in Tocqueville's sense, of the rural poor is closer to that of the British or of the Portuguese in the nineteenth century. I have no doubt where our urban poor stand. It is hard to realize, and perhaps to some people it may even seem wrong to say, that our urban poor often live in conditions that, materially, far exceed those of the rest of the world. But it is the truth.

During the late 1980s, our undersecretary of state for human rights and humanitarian affairs, Richard Schifter, used to have to parry Soviet attacks on America for its poverty and inequality with a strange tactic. He would meet with his Soviet counterpart and actually show him how families on welfare in the United States had television sets, cars, multiple-bedroom apartments, and so on that most "middle-class" Soviet citizens could only dream about.

Schifter was right in material terms, but this raises an interesting comparison that the demise of Marxism now allows us to pursue further. The "condition" of Soviet citizens was also quite bad and alienated, and many of us might have chosen to be a relatively free and happy Portuguese peasant over the grim conditions of Soviet life. But what of the "condition" of our own poor today or our rich for that matter? Because the "condition" of the rich may be equally a question almost entirely independent of their material welfare.

Let me approach this question from what may seem, at first, an odd tangent. Alasdair MacIntyre suggested years ago that the barbarians are upon us and have entered the gates.[7] What we may now be waiting for, he said, is another and quite different Saint Benedict to establish the moral equivalent of modern monasteries to help us survive a new dark age. But until the barbarian horsemen are actually in control of the cities, something that has partly occurred in all the major metropolitan centers of the nation, I am not prepared to give up without a fight. And the fight must go on in the cities because, as every general knows, when you capture the major towns, the countryside will follow.

We have, built in to our American tradition, a good deal of skepticism about cities and the kinds of morals to which they give rise. Jefferson is the fountainhead of this thinking. He expected that if we ever allowed ourselves to be lured off the land and engaged in manufactures, which he preferred we buy from Europe, we would become embroiled in the same urban mess that Europe had. Perhaps he was right and perhaps there is no hope for us in modern urbanized America.

But if we are going to save the current situation, we must save cities as cities. Our postmodern "condition" suggests that living on the land will not be a viable future, not only for Americans, but for much of the human race. Flight to the suburbs, it seems to me, only postpones the problem. If we are to restore real citizenship and civic culture, we need to restore the city. To me, it is a great disgrace that Washington, D.C., the capital of the most powerful and one of the most admirable nations in the history of the world, is also currently in contention for the title of per capita murder capital of the world.

Any clear-sighted look at the cities leaves us feeling we cannot be optimistic.

But the theological virtue of hope must inform our political deliberations, even if we are not optimistic.

Rudolph Giuliani, the mayor of New York, proposed that X-rated businesses be removed from residential and commercial areas and be prohibited from being within five hundred feet of residences, churches, schools, or *one another*. This last qualification is particularly important because, as we all know, an otherwise thriving area may be able to tolerate one sleazy establishment, or even more than one if they are spread out. Concentrating them in a restricted space invites complete destruction of the neighborhood through mutually reinforcing disorders.[8]

In the second half of the nineteenth century, both England and America faced and solved some of the same problems we think most characteristic of our own time. Earlier, alcohol and drug abuse had become rampant in both societies. Urbanization, massive immigration, and the rise of new industries seemed to have unsettled all the old social bonds, with increases in crime and other social pathologies similar to those we see today. The response, which came from both social and religious leaders, was to establish new codes of behavior and fight vigorously against public acceptance of decline. According to the best evidence, and criticism of Victorian hypocrisy notwithstanding, it worked.[9]

Let me suggest, then, some steps that I believe would help us to restore America's cities and in the process its citizens, conceptions of citizenship, and civic culture: First, the founding and the constitutional guarantees of rights to life, liberty, and the pursuit of happiness need to be made functional in every inner city in the United States. Let us be clear what is at stake here. Including inner-city residents in constitutional guarantees is not just another reform project that needs to be worked at. This goes to the heart of what it means to live in a society that promises liberty and justice for all. Central to reestablishing those guarantees is the protection of life and property.

The recent debate over the crime bill, it seems to me, focuses far too little muscle and intelligence on the streets, where they are most needed. Much of the rest of it is simply frivolous. I don't know about anyone else, but whether midnight basketball leagues are available or not, I don't want my adolescent children out at midnight most nights. Our condition calls for other solutions. In jurisdictions such as Houston and elsewhere, for instance, curfews seem to me far more effective responses to the inner-city juvenile crime problem than are recreation programs.

This brings me to a second point. In ways that I believe even Tocqueville could not have anticipated, we now turn far too quickly and hopefully to the complex network of federal regulations to deal with seemingly intractable problems. The framers of the Constitution did not place fighting crime among the federal government's limited powers solely because they believed local responses to various conditions would be a bulwark against overcentralization and tyranny. They also thought that for many issues local jurisdiction was simply more effective. It is easy to understand, given the large share of the revenues that the federal government now routinely takes, why mayors and state governors decide that if everyone else is getting a share of the pie, they might as well, too. But we need to rethink this relationship profoundly and loosen what is virtually a federal stranglehold on local initiatives. If, for example, the Houston curfew is declared unconstitutional by some federal judge on grounds of age discrimination or some other modern shibboleth, we will forfeit a proven and effective way to give people in neighborhoods their liberty and safety for a mess-of-rights pottage.

My third point is that we need federal reform elsewhere as well. I do not expect that this will happen in the near future, but we need serious recasting of welfare and other well-intentioned aid programs. I do not believe that welfare has broken up the inner-city family the way it is sometimes said to have done. Nor do I believe that welfare as a way of life is so attractive that it has stopped people from working. But it has made some choices far less inconvenient than they once were. Inner-city poor families, black and white, are in a crisis, a far greater crisis than the health care system in this country is in. And if we took the measure of what illegitimacy is doing to our cities in terms of poverty, crime, violence, and other not so visible costs, we would have a five-hundred-person task force, working day and night, on that undeniable crisis. That we do not respond to the problem with that kind of vigor says to me and to many in the culture that we are not serious about the problem at all.

I do not intend to go into ways to fix that problem here, but I will propose another proven remedy for some inner-city problems: private inner-city schools. We should not sentimentalize education because many people for various reasons have come to use the term "education" as a kind of mantra to be repeated whenever an urban crisis arises. Absent other changes within cities, even very good parochial schools can only do so much. But even so, they do a lot. If I had one recommendation to make to Catholic bishops and other denominational leaders in America's cities, it would be to start campaigns to open more religious schools and run them at a dead loss if necessary. In most cities with which I am familiar, I don't think the financial loss would persist for long. In fact, almost everywhere, business and community leaders are desperate for ways to rejuvenate inner-city areas and would support new educational initiatives.

Any proposal of this sort would have to face some rather stiff resistance from people who think that promoting alternative modes of education threatens the public schools. This is not an easy battle and there may be many ways that public schools too can be put under more parental and less federal control. But inner-city public schools are failing so miserably at present that we should not sacrifice everyone for the sake of some distant future renewal.

Also, the form renewal aims at in many places has fallen hostage to some less than reassuring educational experts. Take outcomes-based education. As Paul Greenberg recently pointed out, "outcomes" are defined in such vague language that it is impossible not to fulfill them.[10] Furthermore, where, in the past, students had clear goals like learning the multiplication table or the Pythagorean theorem, they now have various goals that mean almost nothing. Missouri has recently come up with 41 outcomes; Ohio, 21 outcomes; Kansas, 10 outcomes, 21 standards, and 53 indicators.[11]

As a parent myself, let me say that I would be happy, under current conditions, if my children learn to read, write, and compute efficiently—and maybe even are exposed to some history, science, and literature so that they have a sense of the rich opportunities America offers to people with skills and drive. (If there are any outcomes, standards, or indicators in this list, I apologize.) But it is clear that there has been no renewal in education because there has been little will to confront the bad momentum that has been gathering in educational circles for decades.

Finally, let me repeat again that those of us who live in the suburbs cannot discharge our duties to the rest of society by paying more taxes to support state programs already in place. The hour is too late for that; we cannot respond to our conditions even through very much larger tax contributions. In a society like ours, our own citizenship status is damaged if we expect to pay others to take care of crucial problems without exerting ourselves in concrete ways.

Our real task now is not to reinvent government or solve the health care crisis. It is not to reform welfare or get tougher on crime. All of these are quite worthy goals, and we may find better or worse ways to do each of them. In my view, our main task is to reinvent the American people. We can do this in several ways, but the common denominator in all of them is to rediscover the reasons for which we undertake all the other piecemeal reforms. I give the last word to the Greek philosopher Plato, who, it seems, faced many of the questions we have been considering in his own time:

> It is not the life of knowledge, not even if it includes all the sciences, that creates happiness and well-being, but a single branch of knowledge—the science of the good life. If you exclude this from the other branches, medicine will remain equally able to give us health, and shoemaking shoes, and weaving clothes; seamanship will continue to save life at sea, and strategy to win battles; but without the knowledge of good and evil, the use and excellence of these sciences will be found to have failed us. (*Charmides*, 174b-d)

Notes

1. See, as one instance among many, "Letters and Essays on Political Sociology," in Marx and Engels, *Basic Writings on Politics and Philosophy*, ed. Lewis Feuer (New York: Anchor Books, 1959), 450–1 and 480–1.

2. Cf. Douglas J. Besharov, "Working to Make Welfare a Chore," *Wall Street Journal*, 9 February 1994, A14.

3. Adams to Jefferson on July 15, 1813, in *The Adams-Jefferson Letters*, II, ed. Lester J. Cappon (Chapel Hill: University of North Carolina Press, 1988), 358.

4. James Q. Wilson, *On Character* (Washington, D.C.: AEI Press, 1991), 28.

5. Ibid., 27–28.

6. These passages from Tocqueville come from *Democracy in America*, II, ed. Phillips Bradley (New York: Vintage Books, 1945), 336–7.

7. Alasdair MacIntyre, *After Virtue* (Notre Dame: University of Notre Dame Press, 1981), 237.

8. A friend tells me, however, that the Catholic Church in Boston responded to a similar situation by asking that the "combat zone" at least be concentrated in one place so that no one would run into pornography without deliberately having sought it out. Different cities, different mores, perhaps, but this only means that the city government should, in any case, try to control forces that inevitably threaten city life.

9. See James Q. Wilson, *The Moral Sense* (New York: Free Press, 1993), 173.

10. Paul Greenberg, "What is OBE and Why is it There?" *Washington Times*, 30 September 1995, C1.

11. Ibid.

8

The Renewal of Civil Society

Gertrude Himmelfarb

One of the things that never ceases to astonish me, as a historian and also as an observer of contemporary affairs, is the rapidity of social change. Historians are supposed to think in terms of the "long run," the deep-rooted, far-ranging, slowly evolving processes of change. We are supposed to look at events from the perspective of eras, of ages, of centuries. In my experience, the relevant unit of time is more often the decade or even the year.

It is astonishing to think back to the electoral campaign of 1992—only four years ago—when the Republicans were derided for raising the social issues and the Democrats rode to triumph on the slogan "It's the economy, stupid." Today both parties are eagerly embracing the social issues, if in different ways. The congressional elections of 1994 have been described as a political revolution. I think one could go even further and speak of them as a social and moral revolution—or at least as the beginning of such a revolution, a recognition that something is very amiss, not only with our government but with our society and our ethos.

I have used the term—it is the title of my recent book—"the de-moralization of society" to characterize our situation. And to see that situation more clearly, I have put it in historical perspective, comparing our society with that of the Victorians a century or so ago. By "de-moralization" I mean not only the familiar sense of that word, the loss of morale, of contentment and good spirit, but also the more serious sense, the loss of morality, of moral bearings and convictions. The latter meaning is reflected in a momentous change in our moral vocabulary—the shift from "virtues" to "values."

Virtues, as the Victorians understood that term (and as the ancient and Christian philosophers did before them), were firm, fixed, and certain. If virtues did not actually govern the behavior of everyone at every time, they were the standards by which behavior was judged. The standards were firm, even if the conduct of the individual did not always measure up to them. And when conduct fell short of those standards, it was deemed to be immoral—bad, wrong, evil—not, as is more often the case today, misguided, undesirable, or (the most recent corruption of the moral vocabulary) "inappropriate."

"Values," by contrast, are relative and subjective. They do not have to be virtues; they can be beliefs, opinions, attitudes, feelings, habits, preferences—whatever any individual, group, or society happens to value, at any time, for any reason. One cannot say of virtues, as one can of values, that anyone's virtues are as good as anyone else's, or that everyone has a right to his own virtues. Only values can lay that claim to moral equality and neutrality. This impartial, "non-judgmental" as we now say, sense of values—values as "value-free"—is now so firmly entrenched in our society that one can hardly imagine a time without it.

The change in our moral vocabulary has been accompanied by a no less dramatic change in our moral behavior. I'll cite only a few statistics to illustrate the contrast between Victorian England and our own time. Illegitimacy at its peak, in 1845, was 7 percent; by the end of the century it had fallen to 4 percent; in East London, the poorest part of the city, it was even lower: 4.5 percent in midcentury, 3 percent by the end. And so with crime, drunkenness, violence, illiteracy, vagrancy. (While the population in this period grew from 19 million to 33 million, the number of serious crimes fell from ninety-two thousand to eighty-one thousand.)

The improvement in the Victorian period contrasts dramatically with the deterioration in our own time. In the past three and a half decades, we have witnessed, both in England and in the United States, more than a sixfold rise in illegitimacy; the rate increased from 5 percent in 1960 to 32 percent today, and gives every indication of continuing to rise. The increase in crime and in the other indices of "social pathology," as it has been called—violence, drug addiction, illiteracy, welfare dependency—have been even more precipitous. And so have been the changes in our attitudes—our "values," as is said. In 1965, almost 70 percent of American women and 65 percent of men under the age of thirty said that premarital sex was always or almost always wrong; in 1972, those figures plummeted to 24 percent and 21 percent—this in only seven years. Until recently, these facts and figures were commonly denied or belittled: they were said to be a product of misperceptions or misreporting, or a reflection of racial and class bias or of an intolerance of diversity and "alternative lifestyles." Today, they are so visible and so egregious that they can no longer be denied, ignored, or explained away.[1]

Nor can one attribute this de-moralization to the economic and technological changes to which we have been subject in recent years. Here the Victorian experience is especially instructive. If we are going through the trauma of a postindustrial revolution, the Victorians went through the no less traumatic experience of the industrial revolution. In fact, the industrial revolution was far more consequential, for it involved not only an economic and technological revolution but also an urban revolution, a political revolution, and a social revolution. Yet Victorian England went through those momentous changes without experiencing any moral crisis, indeed, with an accession of morality.

We are now, rather belatedly, trying to address the problem of the demoralization of our society. Our first response has been political. Having for so long been in the habit of looking to Washington for solutions to all our problems, we took another look at Washington and decided that it itself was, in good part, the problem—that the social programs and policies emanating from Washington had exacerbated rather than alleviated our problems. "Devolution" thus became the mantra of reform: we should devolve power from the federal government to state and local governments. (In theological circles, this is known as the principle of "subsidiarity": higher authorities should not assume functions that can be performed by lesser authorities.)

There is no question that the federal government is more bureaucratic, more cumbersome, more unresponsive to the needs and wishes of the people than state and local governments. The first and most obvious task of the political reformer is to remove the heavy hand of the federal government, which, as often as not, unwittingly encourages and even legitimizes immoral behavior. This has been patently obvious in the case of welfare policies which often make it more advantageous to remain on welfare than to try to get a job, or income tax policies which actually penalize marriage.

Devolution, therefore, is a necessary step toward reform—but not a sufficient one. For, ultimately, moral responsibility lies with the individual and the institutions closest to the individual. At this point, we may reasonably ask for a further process of devolution—the devolution of power from government at all levels to civil society—to those "associations," as Tocqueville put it, that mediate between the individual and the state: churches, neighborhood groups, philanthropies, private schools, civic and cultural institutions, and, most of all, families. It is in these groups that we may expect to find the traditional civic virtues: duty, charity, civility, neighborliness, self-discipline, and social discipline.

This stage of devolution is called for, because just as the federal government has usurped the functions of state and local governments, so state and local governments have usurped the functions of civil society. With the enormous expansion of the welfare system, for example, private charities and philanthropies have been relegated to a secondary and marginal role. So, too, families have been relieved of the obligation of caring for their aged or incapacitated members, thus loosening the bonds not only of familial responsibility and duty but of familial affection and sentiment.   And communities can no longer stigmatize behavior—illegitimacy, for example—that the government subsidizes and thus, in effect, legitimizes. The revival and reinvigoration of civil society is therefore an eminently desirable goal.

Desirable and necessary—but, again, not sufficient. For civil society, alas, has not been immune from the de-moralization that has affected the culture as a whole. The fact is that Americans have always had, even in the worst of times, a strong civil society—not always a good civil society, but a strong one. In the past three decades, while we have been bedeviled by all the problems encapsulated in the term "social pathology," we have witnessed an expansion and proliferation of the institutions of civil society: philanthropies and foundations of every description (and some of unprecedented wealth), private schools and colleges, local newspapers, local television cable stations, radio talk shows, research institutes, think tanks, cultural organizations, public service agencies, and religious institutions (new-age and old).

Civil society has been described as "the immune system against social disease."[2] But civil society itself has been infected by the same viruses that produced those diseases. The educational experiments and theories, for example, that have been so damaging to our educational system (affirmative action, multiculturalism, self-esteem programs, the cultivation of social skills in place of knowledge) were initiated and promoted by some of the most influential institutions of our civil society—universities, foundations, learned societies. The most controversial projects funded by the National Endowment for the Arts (Maplethorpe, for one) have been proudly exhibited in local museums supported by the cultural elites of those communities. Local cable channels bring hard-core porn into the living room. And even churches (mainstream as well as new-age churches) contribute to the narcissism and self-indulgence of the culture.

Nor have families, the bedrock of civil society, been immune from the virus of moral disarray. When Senator Moynihan warned us of the breakdown of the black family thirty years ago, the black illegitimacy rate was just under 25 percent. Today the white illegitimacy rate is almost that (and the black is two and a half times that). If there are fewer unwed mothers in the white middle-class suburbs, there is no lack of divorce, transient "relationships," neglected or over indulged children, and households in which the main cultural vehicle is television, transmitting its incessant messages of sexual promiscuity and violence.

Moreover, civil society itself has been so fragmented and polarized in recent years, as a result of multiculturalism, affirmative action, feminism, and the race/class/gender divisions that dominate so many of our institutions, that there is little coherence or commonality left in that society. Instead of being a common ground for the working out of common problems, civil society has become an arena of warring interests and groups.

It is not enough, then, to revitalize civil society, in the sense of devolving power from the government to civil society. We must also reintegrate it, so that the institutions reflect common interests and serve common purposes. And, even more important—and far more difficult—we must remoralize civil society.

Here, too, the Victorian experience may be helpful. For this is the most memorable example in modern times of a society that has been remoralized. That remoralization is evident not only in the striking improvement of morals and manners in the course of the nineteenth century—a period, as I have said, of great economic and social turmoil—but also in the dramatic contrast between Victorian England and Restoration England.

The remoralization of Victorian England had its roots in the Wesleyan revival in the mid-eighteenth century and in the "moral reformation movement," as it was then called, sponsored by the Evangelicals later in the century.

Wesleyanism was remarkable in several respects. From the beginning, it was as much a movement for moral as for religious reform—as much an ethic as a creed. And the ethic itself had two aspects: the old individualistic Puritan ethic of work, thrift, temperance, self-reliance, and self-discipline; and a social ethic of good works and charity. The Wesleyans established societies for the care of abandoned children, destitute governesses, shipwrecked sailors, and penitent prostitutes; they founded schools, hospitals, and orphanages; they led the movements for prison reform, the abolition of the slave trade, child labor laws, and factory and sanitary regulations. And they did all of this as a religious as much as a moral obligation.

The other remarkable aspect of this religious-cum-moral revival was the fact that it affected all classes of England. After Wesley's death in 1791, one faction, the Methodists, left the Church of England to form their own dissenting sects, while another, the Evangelicals, remained in the established church. The Methodists appealed primarily to the working and lower middle classes; the Evangelicals, to the middle and upper classes. But whatever their social and theological differences, they shared a common ethic that transcended both class and sectarian lines. And political lines as well; it was as much the ethic of the Chartists and Socialists as of the Liberals and Conservatives. (It is often said that the Labour Party was born in the chapel.)

In the course of the century, the religious impulse, especially among the educated, became somewhat attenuated. But the moral fervor remained; indeed, it was intensified, as if to compensate for the loss of religious zeal. This secular ethic expressed itself most dramatically in George Eliot's famous dictum: God is "inconceivable," immortality "unbelievable," but duty nonetheless "peremptory and absolute."[3]

It was this ethic—born of religion and retaining, even in its secularized form, all the authority and passion of religion—that preserved the moral character of England in a period of intense economic and social change. And not only the moral character of the people but the social habits and institutions that constitute what we now call civil society: the family (presided over, as Disraeli said at the time, by the "Royal Family"), neighborhoods, churches, self-help groups, and a myriad of voluntary societies and philanthropies.

Elie Halévy, the great French historian of Victorian England, wrote seven volumes to account for "the miracle of modern England": the fact that England was spared the bloody political revolutions that convulsed the Continent.[4] But underlying that miracle was another: the fact that England was spared the moral revolution that might have been expected in a time of rapid economic and social change.

"Morality is not yet a problem," Nietzsche wrote in 1888. But it would become a problem, he predicted, when the people discovered that without religion there was no morality. The "English flatheads" (his sobriquet for George Eliot and John Stuart Mill) thought it possible to get rid of the Christian God while clinging all the more to Christian morality. They did not realize that "when one gives up the Christian faith, one pulls the right to Christian morality out from under one's feet."[5]

A century later, morality is indeed a problem, perhaps our most serious problem, for a host of reasons—economic, technological, social—that even Nietzsche could not have foreseen. But foremost among them is surely his explanation: the death of God and the death of morality. In retrospect, one might say that Victorian England, and Victorian America, were living off the moral capital of religion, and that post-Victorian England and America, well into the twentieth century, were living off the capital of a secularized morality. Perhaps what we are now witnessing is the moral bankruptcy that comes with the depletion of both the religious and the quasi-religious moral capital.

Today the question that insistently confronts us is: What are the prospects for a moral reformation of society? I've just read a seventy-odd-page transcript of a symposium held recently on just this subject, deploring the present condition of civil society and casting about for ways of improving it. The most memorable thing about this symposium is the fact that twenty or so very intelligent people, who had made this the focus of their thoughts and activities for many years, managed to discuss the subject without ever mentioning religion—not religion in its historical context, or even in its current one, as exhibited in the Christian Coalition, for example.

To a historian this omission is remarkable. If we look to the past for examples of such a moral reformation, the most obvious one is Christianity, which insinuated itself into the Roman Empire at the height of its decadence. Or there is the Protestant Reformation, directed against what it saw as a corrupt Catholicism. Or the Wesleyan revival, reacting against the libertinism of Restoration England. Or the periodic Great Awakening movements in the United States, seeking redemption in what was thought to be an irreligious and dissolute society.

It is no accident that all of these were religious-cum-moral movements. Nor is it an accident that the "Puritan ethic"—which incorporates such secular virtues as work, thrift, temperance, responsibility—comes to us with that religious label. Whatever the philosophical rationale for a purely secular ethic, the fact is that historically the most important movements of moral reformation originated as religious movements.

Until a few years ago, one might have thought that an age as resolutely secular as ours could not sustain a serious religious movement. The emergence of what is called the "religious right" should give us pause. The name is deceptive. It suggests a greater homogeneity than actually exists, and it obscures the extent to which the movement seeks moral as well as religious revival. But the phenomenon itself is undeniable, as politicians in both parties have become acutely aware. Even the media has had reluctantly to pay attention to the mass meetings, in city after city, of "Promise Keepers": fifty thousand or more men assembled for an entire day of prayer, pledging themselves to marital fidelity and familial responsibility—and paying for the privilege of doing this.

It is tempting to compare this to the open-air meetings where the Wesley brothers preached and gained converts. But that was 250 years ago, and a historian is wary of all analogies, let alone those remote in time. What is not so remote, however, is Victorian England. And what is especially instructive for us about that experience is the way morality was infused into all aspects of public as well as private life, and the way people of diverse views joined in that common moral purpose. Thus utilitarians and Evangelicals, worlds apart philosophically and theologically, shared the same moral principles and cooperated on reforms designed to implement those principles.

The current religious revival may well turn out to be confined to a small minority, not only in its inception, as all such revivals are, but even in its later stages. Yet it may prove to be—again, like all such revivals—disproportionately important in the public life of the country. And it may be all the more important if, following the example of the Victorians, it finds common cause with secularists on crucial moral and social issues.

This is already happening, as secular and religious conservatives (and religious conservatives of all denominations) unite in sponsoring reforms designed to strengthen the family, curb illegitimacy, and deter violence and crime. They are even beginning to cooperate on such religious issues as prayers in public schools or public funds for religious schools. And they all look to civil society for a revitalization and remoralization of social and moral life.

But not to civil society alone. For what we have learned, from the Victorians and from our own experience, is that we must bring all the resources of society—religious and secular, private and public, civil and governmental—to bear upon our social problems. A revitalized and remoralized civil society is an essential part of this process of reformation, but so is a genuine reform of governmental policies and agencies. The ethos of a society is not only reflected in its public policies; it is itself shaped by those policies.

A reform of the welfare system designed to discourage welfare dependency, or of the criminal justice system to deter criminality, or of the public education system to raise the level of instruction and improve discipline in the schools, or of the taxation system to favor (rather than, as is presently the case, to disfavor) marriage, would have moral and social repercussions far beyond those systems. For it would substantially affect the quality of our lives in ways we can only begin to appreciate—and perhaps also in ways we cannot entirely anticipate.

It is often said that one cannot legislate morality. Yet we have done just that.

The civil rights legislation of the 1960s proscribed racial discrimination not only legally, but morally as well. Individuals, families, churches, and communities do not operate in isolation, and cannot long maintain values at odds with those legitimated by the state and popularized by the culture. Values, even traditional values, require legitimation. At the very least they require not to be illegitimated. And in a secular society, legitimation and illegitimation are in the hands of the law and government, as well as society and the culture.

Those concerned for the health of civil society have political as well as civic responsibilities. They have not only to abolish those laws and policies that have weakened or illegitimated traditional values. They have to promote laws and policies that will strengthen and legitimate those values. Legislators and policy-makers are as much our moral instructors as are preachers and teachers.

In remoralizing civil society, we must also remoralize our rhetoric. We might start by eliminating the euphemisms that obfuscate our thinking and distort our policies: "welfare," for example, in place of relief; or "sexually active" for promiscuous; or "alternative lifestyles" for single-parent families; or "delinquency" for juvenile criminality; or the department of corrections for the department of prisons; or all the other euphemisms designed to create a "value-free," "nonjudgmental" language. (When I was working on my book *The De-Moralization of Society*, I asked a government agency for the latest statistics on illegitimacy, and was sharply rebuked; the preferred terms, I was told, were "non-marital childbearing" or "alternative mode of parenting." Even "out of wedlock" is now considered too invidious.)

This nonjudgmental, nonmoralistic language is based on the assumption that there are no moral problems; there are only economic, social, racial, or political problems. It is also associated with the view that society is responsible for all social problems so that the "victims" of society cannot be judged adversely. Above all, it reflects the prevailing spirit of relativism, which makes it difficult to pass any moral judgments upon any person or upon any kind of behavior. In fact, this neutral language is not at all neutral. To speak of illegitimacy, for example, as an "alternative mode of parenting" is to legitimize illegitimacy—to legitimize it morally as well as legally.

We are now confronting the consequences of this moral relativism. Having made the most valiant attempt to "objectify" all social problems, to see them as the product of impersonal economic and social forces, we are discovering that the economic and social aspects of those problems are inseparable from the moral and personal ones. And having made the most determined effort to devise policies that are "value-free," that do not stigmatize illegitimacy, for example, we now find that these policies imperil both the moral and the material well-being of their intended beneficiaries.

If we can restore the language of morality, we may also be able to revive such concepts as discipline and self-discipline, and even such archaic ideas as virtues and vices. And if we can remoralize social discourse, we may be able to begin to remoralize social policy as well as civil society.

We are already witnessing the first signs of such a remoralization. The appearance of William Bennett's *The Book of Virtues* on the best-seller list for well over a year is one such sign. (When Bennett first proposed that book, his publisher demurred at the title; "The Book of Values" is what he wanted to call it. Bennett was adamant—and, of course, brilliantly vindicated.) Then there was a past cover of *Newsweek*, emblazoned with the word "Shame," and below it the question "How Do We Bring Back a Sense of Right and Wrong?"[6] To find that on the cover of *Newsweek*, not a notoriously reactionary journal, may be taken, even for an inveterate pessimist like myself, as the harbinger of a new dispensation.

Notes

1. See Gertrude Himmelfarb, *The Demoralization of Society: From Victorian Virtues to Modern Values* (New York: Alfred A. Knopf, 1995), 222–28, 236.

2. Dan Coats, "Can Congress Revive Civil Society?" *Policy Review* (Jan–Feb 1996), 25.

3. Gordon S. Haight, *George Eliot: A Biography* (Oxford: 1968), 464.

4. Elie Halévy, *A History of the English People in the Nineteenth Century*, I, *England in 1815*, tr. E. I. Watkin and D. A. Barker (London, 1924), 387.

5. Friedrich Nietzsche, *Twilight of the Idols*, in *The Portable Nietzsche*, ed. Walter Kaufmann (London, 1976), 515–16.

6. *Newsweek*, 6 February 1995.

9

Religion and the
Secular Retreat from Modernity

Russell Hittinger

Four years ago, the Supreme Court handed down its most recent installment in a long train of school prayer cases. The case, *Lee v. Weisman* (1992), originated in Providence, Rhode Island. Robert E. Lee, principal of a middle school, invited Rabbi Leslie Gutterman, of the Temple Beth El in Providence, to deliver prayers at the 1989 graduation exercises. Such invocations and benedictions were a long-standing custom. The rabbi's prayers were in accord with the standing guidelines, which required that prayers be composed with "inclusiveness and sensitivity." In the invocation, the rabbi addressed the "God of the Free, Hope of the Brave." In the benediction, he expressed gratitude to God as "Lord," for "keeping us alive, sustaining us and allowing us to reach this special, happy occasion." Daniel Weisman, father of one of the graduates, sought a permanent injunction barring Lee and other principals from inviting clergy to deliver invocations and benedictions at future graduations. The district court enjoined the schools from continuing the practice on grounds that it violated the establishment clause. The court of appeals affirmed. On writ of *certiorari*, the Supreme Court heard the case. Justice Kennedy, who delivered the opinion of the Court, ruled the prayer unconstitutional .

Judicial opinions typically contain both reasons of law and dicta. Reasons of law constitute the laws and doctrines which control and, ultimately, resolve the case. Dicta, on the other hand, include things which are said "in passing" about facts, circumstances, and, indeed, about anything that might strike the fancy of the judge. In the case of *Lee v. Weisman*, the dicta are especially telling about judicial perceptions of religion.

For example, Justice Kennedy asserted that while public prayer might be acceptable if "it affected citizens who are mature adults," the state could not responsibly place "primary and secondary school children in this position." The justice might just as well have been speaking of municipal ordinances regulating cigarette vending machines, or "adult" literature. Moreover, he maintained that graduation prayers suggest to school children that "human achievements cannot be understood apart from their spiritual essence," and therefore drain secular events of their ordinary meanings—or in any case, the meanings which the children wish to confer upon the events. For his part, Justice Souter observed that public prayer might be tolerated if conveyed over an "impersonal medium" like a radio; that is, so long as it is directed "at no one in particular" and so long as the impressionable minds of the youth are not affected. In fact, Souter contended that Rabbi Gutterman's prayer was politically and legally suspect merely because it was theistic rather than nontheistic, and thus tended to erode the self-image of children who subscribe to nontheistic prayer. Concurring in the result of the case, Justice Blackmun went so far as to opine not only that religion is socially and politically divisive, but that it tends to make some people homicidal. As evidence for this opinion, he cited an ACLU report on death threats made against judges who render opinions in prayer cases.

I was so intrigued by these dicta that I decided to survey the Court's religious case law over the past four decades, attending only to the dicta. I asked the following questions:

- What is religion, and what distinguishes it from other cultural beliefs and practices?
- What kind of value is it?
- Why ought there to be a legal barrier between religion and government?

I came to the conclusion that a cultural anthropologist, looking only at the Court's dicta, would have good reason to conclude that religion is something that belongs in the category of dangerous poisons or mental illnesses.

I shall not rehearse all of my findings here.[1] Rather, I want to focus upon one particular dictum in *Lee v. Weisman*—one which speaks volumes about the state of religion in our culture. Attempting to answer, for purposes of law, what religion is, Justice Kennedy remarked: Religion is the conviction that "there is an ethic and a morality which transcend human invention." That same term of the Court, Kennedy also wrote in *Planned Parenthood v. Casey* (1992): "At the heart of liberty is the right to define one's own concept of existence, of meaning, of the universe, and of the mystery of human life. Beliefs about these matters could not define the attributes of personhood were they formed under compulsion of the State." These two dicta suggest that a secular sphere of liberty exists in which the human mind invents or constructs meanings, and a religious sphere in which truths and meanings have some status or ground independent of the human mind. Given the Court's interpretation of the establishment clause, it would seem to follow that religion ought to be separated from the public sphere because religion involves the conviction that moral duties (or at least some moral duties) are not the mere artifacts of the human mind and culture. Clearly, Justice Kennedy's opinion that graduation prayers deprive secular events of their meanings means that public prayer in the vicinity of impressionable children robs them of their liberty to construct their own meanings of reality, values, and so forth.

Justice Kennedy's remarks about the value or dis-value of religion in public exemplify a profound reversal of the modern relationship between religion and the public culture of law, politics, and education. Whereas two centuries ago religion was to be separated from the coercive powers of the state because religion was deemed sectarian and irrational, today religion is to be separated from the public sphere precisely because it holds that there is a secular order of propositional truth which is not the mere artifact of a human mind.

Kennedy's dictum points to the existence of a deeper cultural pattern of reversal. In the closing decade of the twentieth century, it is religious people who tend to embody convictions about the priority of propositional truth, science, the rule of law, and the universality of rights; secularists, on the other hand, tend to embody precisely those traits of religion which the Enlightenment thinkers thought so dangerous—traits of mind and culture which today we would call "postmodern," that is, generally, the authority of the mind to construct its own meanings. I want to think through the nature and implications of this reversal. How religious authorities respond to this reversal will perhaps be one of the most significant stories of the next century.

Briefly put, my thesis is the following: Having once separated religion from the public sphere, the intelligentsia of our public institutions have consigned more and more to the religious sphere, including propositions about truths which are essential to a secular order of government. Yet when fundamental truths about morality and justice are consigned to the private sphere of religion, it would seem that only religion will have the authority to govern—if, indeed, we continue to believe that governance must be based on grounds other than brute force.

The Enlightenment intelligentsia defined modernity in terms of a very specific kind of emancipation: namely, the emancipation of the human mind from institutions which were formed around superstition. What is superstition? It is ignorance of causes. Whatever their differences over particular issues of philosophy, such thinkers as Spinoza, Hobbes, Hume, Voltaire, Feuerbach, and Freud all insisted that it was in the very nature of religion to substitute fantasy for reality. Hobbes perhaps made the point most succinctly:

> From this ignorance of how to distinguish Dreams, and other strong fancies, from Vision and Sense, did arise the greatest part of the Religion of the Gentiles in time past. If this superstitious fear of Spirits were taken away, and with it, Prognostiques from Dreams, false Prophecies, and many other things depending thereon, by which, crafty ambitious persons abuse the simple people, men would be much more fitted

than they are for Civil Obedience.[2]

For Enlightenment thinkers, religion is a childish condition wherein the human mind fails to distinguish dream from reality, spirits from the empirical train of cause and effect, and above all, prophecy from the legitimate ordinances of the state. At least in its traditional forms, religion is the soil for undisciplined passions, which wreak havoc not only upon the development of the useful arts and sciences, but especially upon political order. Never mind the fact that many of these philosophical critics of religion were not successful in showing how the mind is connected to anything other than itself. Here, I only report their standard critique of religion. Religion is at once an arrogant and an ignorant refusal to submit to reality. In place of religion, they recommended the knowledge of causes: either the causes of physical nature, or the causes embedded in the social world, or the causes at work in the interior world of psychology.

Despite their remorseless criticism and ridicule of religion, most of the Enlightenment thinkers were cautious about effecting remedies for the religious condition. Marx was an exception; most critics of religion understood that society remained religious and would remain so for the foreseeable future.   Indeed, Western and, in particular, American culture remained religious well into our own century. When people got sick, they prayed. We need only read the diaries and accounts of the American Civil War to verify this fact. This was the generation that invented the first submarine, transported troops via railroads, and used repeating rifles, telegraphs, and photography. Yet these men and women still viewed the world theologically. By and large, past critics of religion understood their own culture. Nevertheless, these critics believed that however stubbornly religion persists in the culture, it must be separated from, or made subordinate to, the state. The warrants for propositions about public things have to be clearly distinguished (both intellectually and institutionally) from warrants for the truth or falsity of propositions about religious things. Again, with the exception of the Marxist states, this separation was never neat and clean; it was never fully effected. But it was the regulative ideal of the modern, constitutional democracies.

Once religion was deprived of the epistemic warrants for governing men in the public sphere, it was necessary to try to make sense of how it functions in the private sphere. Forced to relinquish religion's claims to the public order of propositional truths, theologians defended religion on the subjective grounds of piety. Take, for example, one of the most influential Protestant theologians of the nineteenth century, Friedrich Schleiermacher. In *On Religion: Speeches to Its Cultured Despisers* (1799), Schleiermacher wrote: "In order to make quite clear to you what is the original and characteristic possession of religion, it resigns, at once, all claims on anything that belongs either to science or morality. Whether it has been borrowed or bestowed it is now returned."[3] "Only when piety takes its place alongside of science and practice as a necessary, an indispensable third" can the value of religion be appreciated.[4] For many religionists and irreligionists alike, this attitude represented an acceptable modus vivendi. Religion can be credited with aesthetic and therapeutic value, so long as it recognizes the secular authority in matters of science and justice.

On our shores, the same point was made by William James, who certainly thought of himself as a defender of religion. (He is also a frequently cited authority in Supreme Court dicta.) In *Varieties of Religious Experience* (1902), James insisted that in order to take an accurate measure of the value of religion, it is necessary to distinguish authentic religion, which consists of "feelings, acts, and experiences of individual men," from the domain of propositional truths.[5] Propositional truths about what? Truths about morality and credal propositions about God. Religion consists of passions, dreams, paranormal experiences. Its childishness is therapeutically healthy, so long as it relinquishes claims to an authoritative order of truths governing human conduct. This view of religion contained many of the most salient characteristics of what we today call "postmodernism":

- The notion that the private "self" can achieve health by construing reality as he pleases
- The withdrawal from the discipline of propositional truth, and from the authority of texts and disciplines of interpretation
- The blurring of lines which distinguish what belongs on the inside and the outside of the "self"
- The desire for an escape from the authority of science
- Above all, the refusal to join religious experience with moral truth

In short, much of what the Enlightenment thinkers feared about religion was given a new habitat in the private world of religious experience. Religion was an acceptable participation in the primitive aspects of consciousness eschewed by the high culture.

Many religionists refused to bite on this apple. Catholicism certainly never did. Within Protestantism, denominations were factionalized into liberal and orthodox or fundamentalist camps. The orthodox and fundamentalist camps continued to hold that religion consists of propositional truths, which govern human conduct and which are not completely discontinuous with truths governing the public sphere. The battles over modern biblical scholarship and over the status of Darwinian science make no sense unless we credit fundamentalists with the desire to hold onto Christianity as true, and not merely as a therapeutic option servicing the private psyche.

A Hobbes or a Freud would contend that the assertions of the fundamentalists have no evident foundation in reality; that their claims can be shown to be ignorant of the order of causes, or at least ignorant of the disciplines and methods by which this order must be judged. Today, however, the disagreement is on other terms. And in fact a profound reversal has occurred. The elite culture, and to a significant extent, the popular culture as well, is unsettled by the fact not that religion makes unverifiable claims about truth, but rather that it makes truth claims in the first place—even concerning secular matters, and even about propositions which have no apparent dependence upon revelation. Whereas at one point in our history, religion was criticized and kept at bay because it was deemed a childish withdrawal from the wide-awake world of adult rationality, today it is feared because it advocates the authority of reason. Dan Quayle, we can recall, was ridiculed for daring to contradict the lifestyle choices of a television character.

Having consigned religion to the transrational private sphere of personal experience, it now seems that postmodern culture can't have enough of it. This irony is nicely captured by the history of one prominent family. Thomas Huxley, the famous British zoologist, was best known for his defense of Darwinian science against religious believers. He was the very epitome of hard-headed scientific positivism. Two generations later, his grandson, Aldous Huxley, was internationally renowned for advocating the use of hallucinogenic drugs as the gateways, or as he put it, the "doors of perception," into primordial religious experience. At least for the Huxleys, the Hobbesian distinction between dreams and reality was ultimately resolved in favor of dreams. For Aldous Huxley, science reaches its *telos* by liberating the mind from the constraints imposed by science itself. We are well aware of whose side the 1960s generation took in this matter. It sided with Aldous Huxley not only in matters of religion, but also in the estimation of the authority of science.

For our purposes, the point that I want to make is that the Enlightenment's private sphere of religion has gradually expanded, coming to include things which modern thinkers had reserved to the public sphere—particularly, truths concerning science and justice. Let us return briefly to judicial dicta. In *Webster v. Reproductive Health* (1989), Justice Stevens wrote that "the intensely divisive character of much of the national debate over the abortion issue reflects the deeply held religious convictions of many participants in the debate." Of course, there is no reason to question Stevens's observation that the abortion issue is intensely divisive. Political parties, churches, professional organizations, and the Supreme Court itself are polarized over abortion; it is the very symbol of the so-called culture wars. Yet Justice Stevens simply takes it for granted that the divisiveness over abortion is a symptom of "religious convictions." At issue in this case, among other things, was the preamble to a Missouri statute recognizing the humanity of the fetus. Justice Stevens explains: "Indeed, I am persuaded [of] the absence of any secular purpose for the legislative declarations that life begins at conception and that conception occurs at fertilization." It should be noted that in this case, the statute enacted by the state of Missouri contained no theological propositions whatsoever. It was based entirely upon what the state alleged to be scientific facts of embryology. Stevens, however, swept all before him into the one undifferentiated category of theology. Religion is divisive, therefore, not because it is religious, but because it is audacious enough to use embryological data to support its claim about a matter of justice. Or to put it another way: anyone who would use such data to support a claim about justice is "religious." It is worth recalling that in *Roe v. Wade* (1973), Justice Blackmun declared that the state must remain agnostic about the starting point of human life chiefly because philosophers and theologians themselves disagree about the matter. Why should the laws and policies of the state depend upon debates among theologians? This question cannot be answered without appreciating the cultural reversal we have undergone: we now have religious people arguing facts of embryology against legal authorities who hold that theological debates have proved indecisive.

And so, what began as an effort to consign religion to the private sanctuary of personal piety has become an ever-expanding zone of psychological liberation from the disciplined constraints of the high culture of modernity. This process has been completed by arranging the controversial issues of justice and consigning them to the sphere of religion. Whatever he subjectively intended to say, Justice Kennedy's dictum that religion is the belief in "an ethic and a morality which transcend human invention" hands morality over to religion. To be sure, many religious authorities have either openly or secretly believed that this was always true. Yet it is surprising indeed that the state would make such a concession.

The year 1993 marked the publication of two important documents. First was the appearance of John Rawls's *Political Liberalism*, the long-awaited sequel to *A Theory of Justice*. If there is such a thing as an intellectual authority in liberal political theory, it is John Rawls. The year 1993 also saw the publication of the papal encyclical *Veritatis Splendor.*[6] If we were to rouse Locke, Bentham, and Kant from their graves, they would be surprised and dismayed to discover that the bishop of Rome defends the authority of reason in the political and legal matters of the earthly city, and that the most prominent liberal heir of the Enlightenment insists that public order cannot stand upon propositions of truth.

I want to reflect briefly upon the difference between these two accounts of justice, not only because they exemplify the cultural reversal of our time, but also because they partially explain it. In *Political Liberalism*, Rawls asks: "Given the conflicting comprehensive conceptions of the good, how is it possible to reach such a political understanding of what are to count as appropriate claims?" He continues:

> The difficulty is that the government can no more act to maximize the fulfillment of citizens' rational preferences, or wants [as in utilitarianism], or to advance human excellence, or the values of perfection [as in perfectionism], than it can act to advance Catholicism or Protestantism, or any other religion. None of these views of the meaning, value, and purpose of human life ... is affirmed by citizens generally, and so the pursuit of any one of them through basic institutions gives political society a sectarian character.[7]

Interestingly, what makes for sectarianism, in Rawls's understanding, is not religion per se—certainly not religion in its traditional sense as consisting of creed, cult, and church, but rather any comprehensive doctrine. Rawls emphasizes that although liberalism began by protecting the secular and civil sphere against religious sectarianism, liberalism now must also protect the public sphere against (to use his own words) truths about "human excellence."[8] A stable political order must not only guard itself against the religious fanatic, who believes that all human goods and powers must be subordinated to God, but also against any doctrine that purports to ground the political order in a set of reasons which recommend themselves on the authority of truth. In one fell swoop, all of the intellectual achievements of modernity are dumped into the same category as religion and theology.

Why? Rawls writes:

> Of course, those who do insist on their beliefs also insist that their beliefs alone are true: they impose their beliefs because, they say, their beliefs are true and not because they are their beliefs. But this is a claim that all equally could make; it is also a claim that cannot be made good by anyone to citizens generally. So, when we make such claims others, who are themselves reasonable, must count us as unreasonable.[9]

Rawls therefore proposes that "a distinguishing feature of a political conception is that it is presented as freestanding and expounded apart from, or without reference to, any such wider background."[10] By "freestanding," Rawls means that the political order neither denies nor affirms the truth of such claims as are made by religionists or secularists. Rather, such claims "must count as unreasonable," not because they are adjudged false, but because they cannot be endorsed by everyone; or to put it more accurately, all truth claims have the same warrants of credibility to whoever might privately entertain them. Again: "[T]he fact that we affirm a particular religious, philosophical, or moral comprehensive doctrine with its associated conception of the good is not a reason for us to propose, or to expect others to accept, a conception of justice that favors those of that persuasion."[11] Certainly, Rawls does not deny the existence of authentic truth claims; his point is that they do not count for any public purposes. In fact, to make them count is to act "unreasonably."

Published the same year as Rawls's *Political Liberalism*, the papal encyclical *Veritatis Splendor* takes a quite different position. Pope John Paul II contends that:

> In the political sphere, it must be noted that truthfulness in the relations between those governing and those governed, openness in public administration, impartiality in the service of the body politic, respect for the rights of political adversaries, safeguarding the rights of the accused against summary trials and convictions, the just and honest use of public funds, the rejection of equivocal or illicit means in order to gain, preserve or increase power at any cost—all these are principles which are primarily rooted in, and in fact derive their singular urgency from, the transcendent value of the person and the objective moral demands of the functioning of States. When these principles are not observed, the very basis of political coexistence is weakened and the life of society itself is gradually jeopardized,

threatened and doomed to decay.... This is "the risk of an alliance between democracy and ethical relativism," which would remove any sure moral reference point from political and social life, and on a deeper level make the acknowledgment of truth impossible. Indeed, "if there is no ultimate truth to guide and direct political activity, then ideas and convictions can easily be manipulated for reasons of power. As history demonstrates, a democracy without values easily turns into open or thinly disguised totalitarianism."[12]

While there is plenty of theology in this encyclical, the pope contends that some truths about morality and justice do not depend upon the authority of the Catholic Church. It is one thing to say that a Catholic is required to believe that the church teaches infallibly about morals, but this does not mean that all moral truths require the *religioso animi obsequio*, "religious assent of the soul." Throughout *Veritatis Splendor*, the pope insists that fundamental principles of political morality are found, not in the credal statements of the church, but in the very institutions and practices of constitutional democracy. This encyclical, along with others recently issued by the Vatican, is suffused with the language of eighteenth-century constitutionalism—namely, the language of the inalienable rights of individuals (especially the right of religious conscience), the rule of law, the separation of powers, rights of property, the liberty of economic markets, and so on. But these principles have the authority of reason because human reason itself can know truth. Remove the orientation of the mind to truth, says John Paul II, and we shall have a community in which the "reasons of force" replace the "force of reason." And the pope notes that this is the precise opposite of what democratic institutions "historically intended to affirm."[13]

We cannot help being struck by the fact that, at the end of the twentieth century, the most prominent liberal theorist of the day proposes that the political order must be "freestanding" with regard to moral foundations, while the occupant of the religious office, against which the moderns have so often defined themselves, insists that those moral foundations are sound and must remain in place.[14] Interestingly, this reversal is noted by the pope himself in his most recent encyclical, *Evangelium Vitae*. Referring to state-enforced "rights" of individuals to kill weak or infirm persons, the pope writes: "In this way, and with tragic consequences, a long historical process is reaching a turning-point. The process which once led to discovering the idea of 'human rights'—rights inherent in every person and prior to any Constitution and State legislation—is today marked by a surprising contradiction."[15]

In a recent book on the history of liberalism, the French philosopher Pierre Manent writes: "The motivating force of modern history thus appears to be twofold: the natural desire to escape from the political power of revealed religion; the no less natural desire to escape the mechanism man conceived to satisfy the first desire."[16] If what I have said in this chapter is roughly accurate, the key to the story of modernity is the effort to resolve conflicts over individual liberty and public order by consigning the terms of the debate to the sphere of religion. Hence, we can explain Manent's insight in this way: Not wishing religion to govern, the modern project appears to end by guaranteeing that only religion can govern.

This method of resolving the conflict, by making more and more of it religious in nature, is necessarily subject to the law of diminishing returns. It was one thing to resolve some conflicts between individual liberty and public order by institutionally separating ecclesiastical and civil authority. And, if the truth be known, the framers of modern political institutions were, on the whole, very cautious about how they went about this separation. In our own country, for example, some propositions of civil religion—albeit, constituting only a weak Deism—were left in place. Especially regarding the moral principles of justice, there was not (until recently) an absolute discontinuity between civil and religious truths. The law of diminishing returns is evident when we see the truths which belong, at least partially, to civil rationality being transferred to a merely private religious sphere. Thus, when Justice Kennedy asserts that religion entails the view that "there is an ethic and a morality which transcend human invention," he has, however unwittingly, set in place a dichotomy that makes secular government impossible. Deprived of the warrants of objective truth, the secular government must rule by force; but secular government having capitulated to the notion that objective truth is essentially religious, it would seem that only religion can justify the use of force.

So, we do not have to answer the question about religious influence in a postreligious culture so much as we have to evaluate what it means to live in a postmodern culture in which there are no rational grounds for distinguishing religious and civil truths. Postmodern culture is a culture in which secularism more and more assumes what the moderns regarded as the malign characteristics of religion: the rejection of "logocentrism," and with it, the rejection of the authority of science; the blurring of lines distinguishing institutions of law, education, entertainment, and so forth; the celebration of passions and dreams; the imposition upon the public order of idiosyncratic claims of gender and tribe against the universal claims of human goods and rights; and, in general, an erosion of the principles which once constituted the high culture of modernity. The inner, formerly private world of the psyche is now entitled to impose itself upon the public. Issues of self-esteem and multiculturalist texts on Voodoo in Haiti are deemed acceptable for public education; standards of scientific and mathematical achievement, and substantive principles of morality which purport to be true on some basis other than the constructions of culture, are deemed unacceptable. On the other hand, we cannot but notice that religious authorities more and more take the side of reason, identifying themselves with some of the most basic moral principles of the former high culture. If postmodernism very generally can be defined as a retreat from the authority of science (though not, of course, from applied sciences), it can be defined more specifically in political terms as the retreat from moral truth in the civil sphere.

Whether deserved or undeserved, all of this might appear to be a windfall for traditional religion. At the eleventh hour of modernity, the secular crown jewels have been handed over. I, however, do not think this reversal is a windfall for religion; rather it suggests a terrible burden. For if this transfer of the warrants of truth from the civil to the religious sphere continues unabated, it is difficult to imagine any ending to the story other than religion resuming governance, and this resolution is fraught with dangers.

For instance, to the extent that truth claims regulating justice and policy are transferred from the public to the religious authority, then to that extent the political culture relinquishes principled reasons for the use of force. The liberal might urge society to tolerate a complete dichotomy between the public sphere and the ever-expanding sphere of private truth; but there is not the slightest indication that human beings will tolerate that kind of discontinuity. That is to say, it is unlikely that citizens will live with a government that uses coercive force and yet leaves to mere private estimation the moral truth or falsity which grounds the government action. In this respect, the abortion issue is emblematic of the wider problem. For the Supreme Court never said that the state's estimation of the status and value of the unborn is false; rather, it asserts that it is religious. As the pope points out in *Evangelium Vitae*, common sense rejects the idea that the state should refuse to adopt or impose any ethical position, and at the same time require citizens to be legally bound in conscience to obey the laws. No culture has ever maintained, or even sought to maintain, such a dichotomy.

It is far more likely that the warrants of truth transferred to religion will be reintroduced into the public sphere. This will not occur without controversy: but what principles now govern the resolution of moral, political, and legal controversies? Our political and legal culture has already abandoned clear institutional distinctions between what belongs to civil governance and what belongs to religion—by the very fact of asserting that even the most elementary and commonsensical moral principles belong to religion. In fact, postmodernist culture has no more reliable notion of what does or doesn't belong to governmental authority than what does or doesn't constitute the "selves" who claim rights to construe reality as they please.

The situation seems ripe for religious authority to govern—de facto, if not de jure. Who shall be the candidates? Putting aside all of the secularist and new-age religions, only four religions know how to govern; that is to say, they are based upon propositional truths; they believe that the order of religious truths and the order of moral truths of justice are not completely dichotomous; and at least three of them have hierarchical command structures. They are also the largest and/or fastest-growing religions, not only in North America, but internationally. The four I have in mind are Catholicism, evangelical Protestantism, Islam, and Mormonism. Both Catholicism and Mormonism have institutional memories of theocracy, but both have rejected it in favor of constitutional democracy. It would be most unfortunate if, by default, either of these religions were drawn into a contest over civil power.[17] Evangelical Protestantism has an ecclesiology that favors civil democracy, but we cannot forget that until very recently Protestants still governed the culture. They, too, have an institutional memory of governance. Internationally, Islam has been slow to make the transition to secular political institutions. In fact, in some countries it still incarnates itself theocratically. The moral vacuum created by secularism is liable to prompt a very dangerous response from Islam.

At the same time, our political, legal, and educational elites show little understanding of what they are doing when they hand over moral truth to the so-called private sphere; they seem oblivious to the danger that when they frame public disputes (from teenage sexual continence to educational curricula) in terms of a dichotomy between state-sponsored liberty and moral neutrality on the one hand, and religious authority on the other, they are actually creating a social and intellectual climate in which religion will rule—for by default only religion will have the warrants of truth concerning secular governance.[18] Only religion will be equipped to present and reproduce a rational ground for the institutions of the polity.

Needless to say, this scenario—in which government is the representative of force without moral reason, and religion the representative of moral reason which, ultimately, is the only ground for using force—is undesirable. But we live on the brink of it, over the horizon of our decade. The momentum of the cultural reversal is rapidly moving toward a completion. Two centuries ago, the champions of reason supplied the principles for public institutions, while the old religion held sway over the mores of the culture. Today, religious authorities make the case for reason in the public order, while moral relativism holds sway over the popular culture. The symmetry of this reversal is as fascinating as it is ominous.

The question now is how religion and its authorities will respond. Will religious authorities find a way to resupply the culture with the essential propositions of truth without accepting, by default, the powers of civil governance?

Notes

1. See Russell Hittinger, "The Court's Phobia of Religion," *The World and I* (May 1993): 379–91.

2. Thomas Hobbes, *Leviathan*, §ii.

3. Friedrich Schleiermacher, *On Religion: Speeches to Its Cultured Despisers*, trans. John Oman (New York: Frederick Ungar Pub. Co., 1955), 27.

4. Ibid., 31.

5. Religion, as James circumscribed the topic, is "the feelings, acts, and experiences of individual men in their solitude, so far as they apprehend themselves to stand in relation to whatever they may consider the divine. Since the relation may be either moral, physical, or ritual, it is evident that out of religion in the sense in which we take it, theologies, philosophies, and ecclesiastical organizations may secondarily grow." William James, *Varieties of Religious Experience* (New York: Penguin Books, 1982), 31.

6. For the idea of comparing these two works, I am indebted to the article by John

Haldane, "The Individual, the State and the Common Good," in 13 *Social Philosophy and Policy*, forthcoming (Winter 1996), and in F. Miller, E. Paul, and J. Paul, eds., *Individual, Community and State* (Cambridge: Cambridge University Press, 1996).

7. John Rawls, *Political Liberalism* (New York: Columbia University Press, 1993), 179–80.

8. "[A moral conception] is comprehensive when it includes conceptions of what is of value in human life, and ideals of personal character, as well as ideals of friendship and of familial and associational relationships, and much else that is to inform our conduct, and in the limit to our life as a whole." Ibid., 13.

9. Ibid., 61.

10. Ibid., 12–13.

11. Ibid., 24.

12. *Veritatis Splendor*, §101.

13. *Evangelium Vitae*, §19.

14. As my colleague Michael Novak said in the first sentence of his Templeton Address: "As we draw near the close of the twentieth century, we owe ourselves a reckoning." I believe that it is very significant that, as the recipient of the most prestigious prize for contributions in the area of religion, Novak would make the centerpiece for his address the issue of truth.

15. *Evangelium Vitae*, §18.

16. Pierre Manent, *An Intellectual History of Liberalism*, trans. by Rebecca Balinski (Princeton: Princeton University Press, 1994), 116.

17. And I do not necessarily mean a contest with one another. As the 1994 Cairo Conference indicated, these religions enjoy a remarkable consensus on many moral matters.

18. Consider the political and policy issues championed by the so-called religious right. With the exception of prayer in schools, almost none have the slightest thing to do with religion in the traditional sense of the term, that is, with whether there ought to be seven sacraments or three, or none at all; whether the soul is saved by faith or works; and so forth. Rather, they concern the quotidian issues of politics, such as crime, school curricula, disciplined limits upon the judicial powers of government, abortion, and euthanasia.

10

Christian Principles and Public Life

T. William Boxx

The crisis of moral disorder and sociopolitical dysfunction in American society is widely recognized. The question for Christianity is, How shall it participate in the work of cultural renewal? To be an effective as well as faithful influence for social renewal, Christians need to approach life in the public sphere with an articulated conception of divine order in earthly life and with a self-awareness of how Christian commitment relates to public society. In a time of vigorous and varied Christian activism in the political arena, and when Christian motivation is ascribed to, or claimed by, perpetrators of dark deeds, a sound presentation of Christian character and principles is all the more crucial. All this invariably demands a degree of reflection on both the foundational traditions of our Christian faith and those of the civic order. Furthermore, it follows that there must be principles of integration if we are not to tacitly lapse either into an unacceptable dualism or into monism, that is, either into a schizophrenic separation between spiritual life and temporal life or into ideological or theocratic imperialism.

This essay will especially draw upon New Testament thought and will apply principles derived from it to life in the public square. This is, therefore, a project on the foundations of Christian culture and worldview.

First Things First: Jesus and the Kingdom

A fundamental message of Jesus was to prepare for the coming of God's kingdom, wherein God would rule, not a restored political king of Israel, as generally hoped. Jesus rejected the temptation of Satan to be a political messiah who ruled over earthly kingdoms (Matthew 4:8–10; cf. John 6:15, 18:36). He rejected being the kind of messiah who satisfies popular needs, represented by turning stones into bread (Matthew 4:3–4). He distanced the religion of Israel from its nationalistic-theocratic longings. Jesus could give Caesar his due (Mark 12:17; Matthew 22:21; Luke 20:25) because God allowed Rome to rule, but that would not be the emphasis for one preaching the kingdom of God: "The time is fulfilled, and the kingdom of God is at hand; repent and believe in the gospel" (Mark 1:15). His was a religious and spiritual message with the focus on interior disposition and moral conduct. Love of God and love of neighbor (universally defined) were the core values, and such devotion in the context of the coming kingdom of God results in totally new commitments with old standards of importance no longer relevant—a beginning to live the kingdom life now in anticipation of its full actualization. The kingdom is in our midst already but is yet to come in fullness.

Jesus called people to aspire to the higher virtues in life, and to transform their attitudes as well as their practices, for it is out of the heart that comes "evil thoughts, fornication, theft, murder, adultery, coveting, wickedness, deceit, licentiousness, envy, slander, pride, foolishness" (Mark 7:21–22). True religious and ethical conduct comes from the right attitudes. Jesus upheld the Commandments but went beyond them. Do not murder but also avoid the kind of anger that leads to illicit aggression. Anger can become all-consuming, and his followers are not to be a people of anger. Similarly, do not provoke conflict by insulting people; look for ways to reconcile with those who have something against you (Matthew 5:21–26). Not only is adultery wrong but so also is the intentional lustful attitude that inspires it (vv. 5:27–28).

Jesus taught his disciples to turn the other cheek, give when asked, go the extra mile, offer cloak as well as coat. Vengeance and retaliation were not to be perpetuated, nor even the common attitude of hating enemies, as if these were the ways to win over persecutors or to resolve conflicts. Rather, win over your opponents by loving them, praying for them, treating them respectfully, as it were. In short, overcome evil with good (Matthew 5:38–45; cf. Romans 12:17–21, and 1 Peter 3:9). And do not be zealously judgmental and self-righteous or look for fault in others as if you had the eyes and authority of God (Matthew 7:1–5).

When Jesus was asked what one needed to do to inherit eternal life, he affirmed the great commandment to love God with all your heart, soul, strength, and mind, that is, your whole being, and to love your neighbor as yourself (Luke 10:27). To the question of just who is my neighbor, he responded with the parable of the good Samaritan, which demonstrates that all people are to be thought of as "neighbors" and therefore owed "mercy" or humanitarian dignity, not just one's religious or ethnic fellows. How do you love your neighbors? By showing them "mercy" (vv. 10:30–37). In the end, all are human beings created by God to whom the obligation of dignity and charity applies. Thus, the religion of Jesus is universalistic in this regard. And as a summary ethic, "whatever you would wish that men would do to you, do so to them" (Matthew 7:12).

Jesus was a teacher of wisdom and a prophetic preacher. His wise and inspiring words pointed people to the kingdom-life he proclaimed, a kingdom that remained to come in fullness, yet flowered in our midst already as the humble mustard seed that grows into the largest of shrubs (Mark 4:30–32). What we hope for and pray for, we aspire to, and, therefore, the sayings of Jesus constitute standards for our personal lives in terms of how we relate to others and God. People formed by hearing the sayings of Jesus would aspire to be slow to anger, long suffering, peaceful, conciliatory, generous, unpretentious, kind to all, and generally virtuous. Followers of Jesus are shaped by this spiritual and moral message, yet prudence also must guide us in the world: "Behold, I send you out as sheep in the midst of wolves; so be wise as serpents and innocent as doves" (Matthew 10:16).

Virtuous admonitions from the Gospels constitute some of the higher qualities of civilized life. Who could not hope that a greater measure of these admonitions' influence be spread, especially in the more turbulent parts of our country and world or in ameliorating the coarser aspects of our culture? Much of what Western civilization holds as constituting the higher values of human life is infused with the moral wisdom of Jesus and has inspired our progress, slow and halting as it has been, throughout the centuries. The message of and about Jesus is a force for good in the world.

The community that emerged after Jesus was a society within society. Indeed, Paul's use of the phrase "body of Christ" for the Christian community recalls the ancient civil usage of "body" as a term for the *polis* or *res publica*, as in "body politic."[1] The resurrection event vindicated the life and death of Jesus and became the founding faith of the new movement. He who preached the kingdom became what was preached about. The Christian community was formed around the missionary preaching of the original disciples of Jesus, prominently Peter, James, and John, and early apostolic missionaries like Paul and Barnabus. Even so, the Christians lived among others and largely abided by the prevailing rules. They showed themselves to be good citizens, as it were, by their virtuous conduct and acceptance of the ruling order.

Christianity and Governing Authorities

From the historical beginnings of the Christian faith, there was an acceptance of the governing authorities of the world under the providence of God. Especially notable are Paul and his mostly Gentile (non-Jewish) communities because they lived under the Roman political order without the special religious-civic arrangements that Palestinian Judaism variously enjoyed. Roman law and order and Hellenistic culture constituted their social context just as American polity and Western civilization (including Judeo-Christian tradition) in general constitute ours. From Paul's perspective, government served a valuable and divinely ordained purpose even in the meantime, that is, until the Parousia, when the return of Christ would fully inaugurate the new creation. Government, Paul declares, is "instituted by God" and is "God's servant for your good." Its fundamental function is to provide law and order and punish wrongdoers: "For rulers are not a terror to good conduct, but to bad." Thus Christians should honor governmental authority and be law-abiding citizens, including paying taxes, and they are conscience bound to do so (Romans 13:1–7). At the same time, the inference is that government is accountable to God and is to serve the common good.

Perhaps Paul's views reflect something of the tradition from the Gospel saying of Jesus, "Render therefore to Caesar the things that are Caesar's, and to God the things that are God's" (Mark 12:17; Matthew 22:21; Luke 20:25). It is certainly in consort with the practice of the temple priests in Jerusalem who made sacrifices *for* (but not *to*, as others did) the Roman emperor. This view also reflects Old Testament and intertestamental understandings of Judaism in exile under foreign dominion. For example, during the Babylonian exile Jeremiah gives a prophecy of God to the elders and leaders who were formerly of Jerusalem to "seek the welfare of the city where I have sent you into exile, and pray to the Lord on its behalf, for in its welfare you will find your welfare" (Jeremiah 29:7).[2] All the more accommodating to the ways of Roman life would be those Hellenistic Jews like Paul who lived outside of Palestine and more directly imbibed Greco-Roman culture. But at heart is the understanding of God's providence in history as the God over all.

Elsewhere in the New Testament, a similar admonition regarding government is expressed in the first letter of Peter (interestingly, written *from* Rome as Paul's letter had been written *to* Rome), where the readers are told to be subject to governmental institutions, which are said to exist to "punish those who do wrong and to praise those who do right." Therefore, the Christians are to "honor the emperor" (1 Peter 2:13–17). Likewise, in the letter to Titus is the admonition to "be submissive to rulers and authorities" (Titus 3:1; cf. 1 Timothy 2:2).

One could also look more generally to the book of Acts of the Apostles, which chronicles the spread of Christianity from Jerusalem throughout the Roman empire to the capital of Rome. A careful reading shows that the author, who addresses his combined work Luke–Acts to a Roman official or nobleman ("most excellent Theophilus"), portrays Christianity as a nonsubversive religious movement that should be tolerated, if not respected, by the Roman government. As a brief sampling: The proconsul Gallio refuses to support Jewish leaders' accusations against Paul at Corinth, declaring that no "wrongdoing or vicious crime" is at issue (Acts 18:14). It is a Roman tribune who saves Paul from the Jerusalem mob and in a letter to the governor declares that Paul has done nothing deserving of death or imprisonment, which certain Jewish leaders of Jerusalem demanded (Acts 23:29). King Agrippa, who ruled under Roman authority, declares the same (Acts 26:31). The trials and reaction to the charges against Paul by the Roman authorities are similar to Jesus' experience before Pilate and King Herod, who did not believe Jesus to be a subversive as the chief priests and scribes portrayed him (Luke 23:1–25). Neither Jesus nor Paul challenged Roman order as such.

At several points in Acts, Paul raises the issue of his Roman citizenship in difficult situations. When local magistrates abuse him and Silas, Paul declares his Roman citizenship and solicits their apology (Acts 16:19–40). When Paul is about to be beaten, he tells the tribune that he is a Roman citizen; he is therefore spared (Acts 22:22–29). And finally, Paul exercises his right as a Roman citizen to appeal to Caesar when it does not seem promising before governor Festus, although Festus subsequently says he would have released him had he not appealed to Caesar (Acts 25:6–12). Thus, in his trials Paul is shown to be a Roman citizen, a respecter of Roman law and no wrongdoer, and such is generally recognized by the governing authorities, although ultimately he would lose his head (not recounted in Acts) at Roman hands.

Now one could say that the rather optimistic tone of the spread of Christianity through the Roman world depicted in Acts and the accommodating political sentiments in Romans, 1 Peter, and Titus fail to anticipate times of official persecution and setbacks and are hardly useful for living in unjust states. Without question, the whole of Christian values, experience, and reason must be brought to bear when dealing with such complex sociopolitical situations; in the end we "must obey God rather than men," as said Peter and the other apostles (Acts 5:29). But one obviously must distinguish between the theological idea that political and civil order is God's will for our good and its various human applications.

In any event, the foundational Christian heritage undeniably contains important ideals about God's worldly order for human governance. From such as the above cited authoritative examples, principles for Christian civic life can be derived. One such basic principle is that the existence of civil government is part of God's design for our well-being. Although Christians are a people whose ultimate "commonwealth is in heaven" (Philippians 3:20) or the kingdom of God, in the meantime we are subject to a divinely ordered world that takes into account temporal order as well as the spiritual. The Christian is to responsibly relate to the political order, rightly construed, as well as the spiritual order, because God's rule extends to both spheres. Another key principle is that government is not absolute; it exists only to serve our good as ordained by God, and it is to be an encouragement to moral behavior.

The Broader Culture

In spite of its eschatological framework, Christianity was not a wholly esoteric or separatist religious cult whose philosophy and public way of life drew exclusively on the mysteries of its divinely revealed story and denied any relation or validity at all to non-Christian learning and culture. To be sure, something definitive and unique occurred in the Christ event, which compelled a totally new commitment (i.e., Jesus is Lord) and envisioned a truly new order of the ages, if you will, and which entailed the compulsion to share the message with the world before the world passed away. The very command to preach the gospel to the nations (e.g., Matthew 28:19) carries within it the presumption that some, at least, in the non-Jewish world would be able to relate to the Christian message through their preexisting cultural worldview, experience, and concomitant reason.

Thus, the Christian message, especially formulated by Paul and his followers, was able to address the culturally framed (Greco-Roman) religious and moral longings of the people. A representative example can be seen in Acts of the Apostles where Paul dialogues with the pagan thinkers of Athens in a way that acknowledges some of their ideas (Acts 17:16–34). Paul began by preaching in the synagogue, then in the agora, that is, the marketplace or public square, where commercial, governmental, and philosophical activities mingled. His preaching piqued the interest of Epicurean and Stoic philosophers, who took him along with them, presumably away from the crowds, to the Areopagus, where the ancient Athenian council once met. Paul's speech employed biblical and philosophical concepts held in common with the schools of Greek thought: disdain for popular superstition and attempts to manipulate the gods "by human hands as though he [God] needed anything" (v. 25); the unity of humanity, with God having "made from one every nation of men" (v. 26); the philosophers' quest to "seek God, in the hope that they might feel after him and find him" (v. 27); the kinship of humanity with God, in that "we are indeed his offspring," which Paul quoted from "some of your poets," specifically, Aratus (v. 28).[3] For all of this, still Paul preached Jesus raised and the time of decision. The result was that some scoffed but some were interested and a few converted.

To some degree, Pauline Christianity incorporated the best of Greco-Roman virtues and could appeal to reason, not just Judeo-Christian revelation. Thus, Christianity was able to attract and persuade those not imbued in the Jewish culture from which it sprang. Christianity necessarily engaged the cultural public arena in a manner that was relevant to the language and ideas of those with whom it was in dialogue. Some of Paul's moral language could have been recited by any Greek philosopher, as in the case of the Stoic virtues he commends to the Philippians: "whatever is true, whatever is honorable, whatever is just, whatever is pure, whatever is lovely, whatever is gracious, if there is any excellence, if there is anything worthy of praise, think about these things" (Philippians 4:8).

Paul often expressed the Christian ethic in such catalogues or lists of virtues and vices in the style of Hellenistic philosophical writings. The inward transformation through faith in Christ removes one from the control of the flesh and its vices and opens one to the life of the Spirit and its virtues. In Pauline thinking, "fleshly" means closed to the spiritual. And the works of the flesh are such as "fornication, impurity, licentiousness, idolatry, sorcery, enmity, strife, jealousy, anger, selfishness, dissention, party spirit, envy, drunkenness, carousing." In contrast, the "fruit of the Spirit is love, joy, peace, patience, kindness, goodness, faithfulness, gentleness, self-control" (Galatians 5:19–23). These are characteristics that mark the life of those who are in Christ, but they are also characteristics which could generally be interpreted as at least tacitly making one a virtuous member of society.

Christians are to carry out their lives in a responsible manner so as to be a burden to no one and to command the respect of all. Addressing the Thessalonians, Paul says: "aspire to live quietly, to mind your own affairs, and to work with your hands, as we charged you; so that you may command the respect of outsiders and be dependent on nobody" (1 Thessalonians 4:11–12). There is here a basis for the work ethic and the respect for community relations which are so important in the social history of our country and which are constitutive for stable social order. Perhaps the Thessalonian community did not sufficiently integrate this ideal into their public life, for the second letter to them elaborates the point in a rather more definitive way:

> Now we command you, brethren, in the name of the Lord Jesus Christ, that you keep away from any brother who is living in idleness and not in accord with the tradition that you received from us. For you yourselves know how you ought to imitate us; we were not idle when we were with you, we did not eat anyone's bread without paying, but with toil and labor we worked night and day, that we might not burden any of you. It was not because we have not the right [i.e., as apostles], but to give you in our conduct an example to imitate. For even when we were with you, we gave you this command: If anyone will not work, let him not eat. For we hear that some of you are living in idleness, mere busybodies, not doing any work. Now such persons we command and exhort in the Lord Jesus Christ to do their own work in quietness and to earn their own living (2 Thessalonians 3:6–12).

If this is a basic ideal for Christian life in society, then when we think about policies for public life, these ideals of personal responsibility should constitute the basis of domestic initiatives to help people. Programs that contribute toward dependency violate human dignity and the ethic of our tradition.

Another important ethic from our tradition with ramifications for contemporary public life flows from a pastoral concern for harmony within the Christian community. In the Corinthian church, members had become grievously argumentative and were taking their disagreements to the secular courts. Paul tells them that it is to their shame "that brother goes against brother" because to "have lawsuits at all with one another is a defeat for you. Why not rather suffer wrong? Why not rather be defrauded? But you yourselves wrong and defraud, and that even your own brethren" (1 Corinthians 6:5–8). The quality of brotherhood as constitutive for community life is here at stake. Paul recommends that such disputes as arise should be handled internally by those among them respected for their wisdom, but clearly the ethic of mutual love should really prevail. The idea of willingness to suffer wrong is perhaps reminiscent of Matthew 5:39–40: "But if anyone strikes you on the right cheek, turn to him the other also; and if anyone would sue you and take your coat, let him have your cloak as well."

One cannot but think of the extensive litigiousness of our society today when reading this passage, although the situations are quite different. Still, if we take this passage as inspiration for us in general, then we should look for ways to promote harmony in society, including in our legal culture. In such a large and complex society as ours, maintaining a general sense of harmony is difficult indeed. What people and their governments at each level can do is to help assure that the laws and public cultures do not encourage a spirit of hostility and opportunism where the least slight or conflict becomes an occasion for formalized action or an excuse for personal gain. It seems that every difficulty or controversy reaches the courts. It is surely a sign of disharmony and weakening social bonds that we have become such a litigious society. The extent of litigation in our society is an uncivilizing condition and a "defeat for us" as a culture and a scandal to the credibility of the rule of law. Our legal culture should be ordered in such a way as to discourage unfounded and excessive legal action without, of course, mitigating the requirements of justice. Certainly self-conscious Christians should be slow in the bringing of personal suits and not perpetuate a coarse political-legal environment. This is also the attitude reflected in Matthew 5:25, where Jesus' followers are encouraged to avoid legal action in favor of private reconciliation.

If Pauline Christianity can sometimes be interpreted as relating to the commendable values of Greco-Roman culture, it may also be perceived as too readily accommodating the negative social structures of the times. Simply put, Paul did not take it as his mission to change the social system within which he lived. One must sometimes look deeper for the inspiration in Scripture to see what principles can serve as lessons for us. Nevertheless, Paul does lay the groundwork for the ecclesial understanding that social distinctions have no status in the body of Christ: "For by one Spirit we were all baptized into one body—Jews or Greeks, slaves or free—and all were made to drink of one Spirit" (1 Corinthians 12:13).

The "house codes" of the deutero-Pauline letters, in spite of their difficulty for modern understandings of justice and equality, demonstrate the relevance of social order in later Pauline Christianity.[4] It would be a disservice to the inspirational nature of Scripture to ignore these passages, but deeper interpretations are required. Still, the ethic of love, respect, and fellowship and a measure of relative equality shine through, especially considering the social structures of the times.

The importance of the family unit formed by husband and wife is particularly apparent, constituted by commitment, mutual love and respect, and disciplined stability. While we do not uphold the rigid patriarchy of the times, still the idea that there are gender and intrafamily distinctions ought not to be anachronistically dismissed. The roles of mothers and fathers are not completely interchangeable. Men and women have differences by nature, and the modern denial of this, along with other ideological anomalies, has led to the "superfluous father" syndrome and other social problems. The epidemic of father absence has undermined the very existence of family life and has led to the social pathologies we now can hardly cope with, especially the violence and irresponsibility of unsocialized young males. The mother-and-father-based family is the basic unit of society, wherein children first learn about love and truth and moral standards. Civilization cannot endure its demise.

Parents have a responsibility to their children, including concern for the kind of society they leave them, "for children ought not to lay up for their parents, but parents for their children" (2 Corinthians 12:14). The reckless disregard for the future, for example, through spendthrift policies, no matter how well meaning, is a fundamental disorder, not just poor financial stewardship, leading to social collapse. The sense of failing our children and burdening their future for our present pricks our conscience. That is what is behind the broad concern about deficit spending and a seemingly uncontrollable government. Added to this uneasiness is the troubling perception of the antivalues in popular culture, the failures of the educational establishment, and divisive political action by groups of various sorts, so that we fear we are laying up only chaos for our children's future.

There is explicit equality in Paul's theology that at first glance seems to challenge the social structures to which he and his successors related. He says quite forthrightly that for Christians "there is neither Jew nor Greek, there is neither slave nor free, there is neither male nor female; for you are all one in Christ Jesus" (Galatians 3:28). This equality refers to all individuals' equal standing before God and their need of God's redeeming grace in Christ. It is a religious equality that embraces the new creation so that all else is secondary in relevance. There is a certain consonance between Paul's sense of equality and Jesus' table fellowship with tax collectors and "sinners" (e.g., Luke 5:29–32). The radical nature of God's kingdom undoes alienating social attitudes and shows that all are equally in need of God's grace.

From our historic perspective, Paul may not seem to follow his concept of equality as far as we would now demand, but there is more to it than meets the eye. For him Christians should live as responsible members of society, even to the point of accepting their difficult stations in life because, for one reason, such social conditions are secondary when compared to life in Christ and the new world to come. Yet Paul is also concerned that Christians should "live peaceably with all," thereby sparing themselves unnecessary troubles, which has much virtue in itself and is certainly a civilizing quality (Romans 12:18). Even if it had occurred to him, Paul could not preach social rebellion and also effectively spread the gospel. And woe to him if he does not preach the gospel (1 Corinthians 9:16), as he says of his compulsion, which remains the primary mission of the church. While still attending to the demands of basic justice, Christians must not allow desire for sociopolitical reform to overwhelm the preaching of the gospel and spiritual nurture.

In their own time and social context, Paul and his successors did well to help people learn to cope with their lives and to encourage the higher values in human relations. The love and respect he admonished on those in socially superior positions was an advance over common cultural attitudes. We can also see in Paul's attitudes the nonretaliatory ethic of Jesus, so that we are to "bless those who persecute you" and "repay no one evil for evil" (Romans 12:14, 17; cf. Matthew 5:38–39, 44, and 1 Peter 3:9). Curtailing the endless cycles of retaliation, vengeance, the making of enemies, and so forth is a quality that we would recognize as constituting a higher and more humane order. Just as the "eye for an eye" ethic was superior to the ancient blood laws wherein many would be harmed in retaliation for the wrong against one. In dealing with difficult issues today,

Christians and the church should approach them realistically in light of the sociopolitical conditions in which they operate. A prudent perspective in the larger context and persuasion to lift current practices to a higher moral plane should be the usual approach. Prudence means making disciplined decisions based upon reasonable perceptions. It is a virtue which recognizes that an excessive drive for perfection impedes progress toward the good and therefore becomes a vice. At worst, perfectionistic approaches become a heretical crusade to, in effect, establish the kingdom of God by one's own work.

In the fullness of time, this Pauline religious equality becomes the basis of ideas about human equality in general when Christians realize that they must more deeply attend to questions of civil society. Because all stand before God equally and all are equally creatures of God, an enlightened Christian society that recognizes this can hardly justify anything but equality before the law within its sociopolitical order, in spite of the grueling graduality of its full actualization. At the same time, we cannot, after two thousand years have passed, operationally assume the imminent end-time as did primitive Christianity. The end comes in God's good time, the times and seasons of which no one knows (Acts 1:7); we must responsibly live and plan as if the world continues, without speculating on God's designs. Thus must we derive key principles in the tradition for life today, remaining faithful to the core Christian vision. The principles behind Pauline theology in these matters are such as the ethic of love, mutual respect, moral virtue, orderly and peaceful relations, responsibility, work, the importance of stable families, and equality before God and all under the rule of God. Such as these can Christians take into society.

The Incarnation of Wisdom and Truth

A Christian sociopolitical order should flow from a foundational theology of the created order and truth. The Gospel and letters of John are another important biblical source for this kind of reflection. The Johannine corpus is characterized by the revelation that Jesus is the Word become flesh. Jesus is the one who has come from above and through whom all things came to be. He is one with the Father. He is the way to truth and life. He is the true revealer.

The Gospel begins with a prologue imitating the Genesis creation account, using the same introductory words: "In the beginning." Christianity now understands creation in a new way, and to express that understanding John uses a term linked to a Greek Stoic concept, *logos* "the Word," which was the principle of reason and order in the universe. This concept had come to be understood in connection with the Jewish theology of divine Wisdom (*sophia*). Philo, a first-century Jewish thinker, had also identified *logos* with Wisdom. In philosophical intertestamental Judaism, Wisdom had come to be thought of as the manifestation of God's creative power, so that it was through Wisdom that God created all things. And Wisdom was also thought to have come down to dwell with humanity, so to speak. While holding to monotheism, one could, nevertheless, speak of Wisdom of in personalistic terms. As a prologue to the Gospel, John uses a *logos* hymn that contains concepts found in Greek philosophy and Jewish philosophy to point to revelation truth, which those of his milieu would now be prepared to more fully understand. Thus: "In the beginning was the Word (*logos*), and the Word was with God, and the Word was God. He was in the beginning with God; and all things were made through him, and without him was not anything made that was made" (John 1:1–3). In a manner of speaking, we may say that the principle of reason is understood to be joined with creation.

Of crucial theological importance is John's incarnational understanding. In spite of the high degree of spirituality in the Gospel, the physical and material cannot be meaningless in a religion whose God "became flesh and dwelt among us" (John 1:14). While John's proclamation of the preexistent Jesus is rightly taken to be the epitome of christology in the New Testament, the point is rather to emphasize his humanness. Christ truly came as a man not just a spirit seeming to have a body. The Word became this real, human Jesus who was historically known in person, "which we have heard, which we have seen with our eyes, which we have looked upon and touched with our hands," as the first letter of John has it (1 John 1:1). From the understanding of the human credibility of Jesus, against those who denied it and broke away from the community of John, there accrues some dignity to humanity in its fullness as well. We are not just spirits trying to escape the entrapment of our bodies as later gnostics held and thereby rendered the conditions of bodily life of no importance. The gnostic view can lead to one of two extremes—inordinate asceticism or libertinism. We are embodied souls or ensouled bodies and part of God's creation. Human life matters in Christianity and thus do provisions to sustain and order life in the world. Gnosticism, which altogether denies the goodness of creation, seeks spiritual escape from the world and renders questions of public life irrelevant, whereas Christianity finds that it cannot avoid them.

An equally important concept in John is the identification of God as truth. God calls us to be truth-seeking people, to realize that there are distinctions to be made among values and ideas about how to live in the world. Not all things can be equally true and good because ultimate grounding of such rests in God. The Spirit of God in the world is the Spirit of truth (John 14:17, 15:26, 16:13). There is such a thing as truth, an absolute that counsels us to discover enduring principles by which to order our lives. The Johannine Jesus says, "you will know the truth, and the truth will make you free" (John 8:32). There is no possibility of real freedom without order and the truth from which it comes. We know only in part and imperfectly (1 Corinthians 13:9, 12), but we know that we live not in a creation of chaos and accident where there is finally no basis for life's judgments but individual will and power. The attitude of limitless variability and relativity that has nothing to do with the truth belongs to the "father of lies" (John 8:44).

Our inferences and extrapolations about Christian life in civil society must be properly weighed in the balance of ultimate concerns. Especially from the community of John we learn that Jesus and his followers are aligned against "the world," which is under the influence of Satan (e.g., John 12:31, 14:18–19, 16:11). They are not "of the world," and the world hates them. Lest we take this interpretation too far, we should recall that Paul too could preach against the world ("do not be conformed to this world," Romans 12:2) while still holding to God's rule in the world and Christian acceptance of civil order. In Jesus' prayer just before his betrayal and passion, he says of his disciples that although they, like him, are not "of the world," he explicitly does not pray that the Father should "take them out of the world." Rather, he prays only that the Father keep them from the evil one (John 17:14–15). And it is in John that we have the famous expression of God's love for the world: "For God so loved the world that he gave his only Son," who, furthermore, was sent "into the world, not to condemn the world, but that the world might be saved through him" (John 3:16–17). The "world" in this sense stands for all that has gone wrong in God's good creation. To adherents of an incarnational religion, being against the world cannot be interpreted to mean hating physicality and nature. Rather, the Christian attitude is "against the world for the sake of the world."

The community of John is especially imbued with the great command of Jesus "that [they] love one another" as Jesus has loved them (John 13:34–35, 15:12) and by the guidance of the Spirit who "will guide [them] in all the truth" (John 16:13). Along with this is a strong desire for unity, which has apparently been fractured and for which Jesus prays "that they may be one" (John 17:11, 21–23; cf. 10:16, 21:11b). Finally, the risen Jesus sends forth his disciples (representing the church) as the Father has sent him (John 20:21). Like Jesus, they will proclaim the God of love and truth, the message of repentance and forgiveness and eternal life. The risen Jesus guides his church in this mission activity, symbolized by the large catching of fish at his direction in the final chapter of the Gospel (John 21:4–6).

The Gospel of John can be taken as a call to us to remember that this spiritual mission is the priority work of the church in the world and that such must be constituted by love, truth, desire for unity, and openness to life led by the Spirit. The primary mission of the church is to proclaim the gospel and spiritual nurture. It is not normally to interject itself into the authority of the state as if it were only "of the world" and ordained for civil rule. To do so threatens to diminish the spiritual and moral credibility of the church and thereby its effectiveness in proclaiming the gospel. Nevertheless, the truth and order derived form the Creator should underlie Christian conceptions of sociopolitical life. Finally, we are reminded that there is yet darkness in the world and our task is not one of accommodation to the evil propensities of the world but rather to be a light in it.

The Civil Order and Reason

Faithful Christian involvement in the civil order must proceed from the basic theological conviction that God created the world and all that exists (the first lines of the Apostles' and Nicene Creeds and the first verses of the Bible and the Gospel of John). Furthermore, as inferred from New Testament sources, it follows that some truths about the Creator and creation can be known through created nature, including reason. Paul implies in Romans 1:18–23 that pagans before Christ could have known God and moral rightness through the created order because such "has been clearly perceived in the things that have been made." To some extent at least, pagans are able to do what the moral law requires because it is "written on their hearts" (Romans 2:14–15). In spite of humanity's fallen state, knowledge of basic moral precepts and ability to search for God, though impaired, are not obliterated. Or, as Thomas Aquinas phrased it, humanity has an "inclination to good" and thus "has a natural inclination to know the truth about God and to live in society," and there follow certain naturally knowable standards.[5]

Concomitantly, active Christian life in society should be guided by a functional theological understanding of the relationship between civil authority and the church. An early church father and expositor of the relationship between Christianity and the *polis,* or "city-state," was Augustine in the fourth to fifth century. While not all aspects of Augustine's thought can be easily incorporated, there are emerging lines of thought which are useful and valid for our consideration today. Augustine was faced with challenge from pagans who blamed Rome's fall on Christianity for having allegedly precipitated the internal weakening of civic tradition. His famous work, *The City of God,* is his response to that charge. He leans significantly on Romans 13 (cited above) as a theological basis for Christian compatibility with civic patriotism. Thus, Augustine's answer is that civic responsibility is compelled by God and expressed in Christian Scripture. Furthermore, Christian teaching promotes moral virtue, which accrues to the benefit of civic life.

The city of God is contrasted with, but to some degree overlaps, the "city of man," and Christians are citizens of both. The city of man, that is, government and civil society, exists to address the temporal and material goods necessary for human life, including law and order, and Christians and the mission of the church are beneficiaries of, and contribute toward, this common good. While the city of man cannot hope to achieve perfect justice and virtue on its own, relative social order and well-being can be established until the city of God is fully manifested by God at the end-time.[6]

In a similar vein, Pope Gelasius, late in the fifth century, famously postulated that the world is ruled by two powers, or "two swords," church and state, which eventually came to be known as the two-kingdom theory or the twofold rule of God.[7] Much later, Thomas Aquinas, who lived in the thirteenth century, would further expound, though in a more nuanced way, the idea of society as governed by two powers, civil and ecclesiastical. Following Aristotle, he held that the purpose of the *polis* and civil society was to provide for the common good, which entailed the promotion of virtue among citizens. Knowledge of human good and right political order in civil society is accessible by reason, but in the end, the norms and laws of civil society are subject to God as revealed by the Christian faith

While it must be said that the spiritual sphere, as entrusted to the institutional church, has a certain ultimate primacy in Thomistic thinking, yet the church should not normally interfere in the rule of the just state. For the state is part of the natural order and governed by human law. Although modern ideas would rightly rebel against the barest hint of any church dominance of government, an important principle can here be inferred—that state power is not absolute and is subject to higher moral and spiritual authority.[8] Government is accountable to ultimate truths as our own American founders so expressed in the Declaration of Independence. And in complementary fashion, the church as an institution should not seek to govern.

Humanity can ascertain something about moral virtue and the common good by reason, and such is an intrinsic aspect of our created nature. Belief in the Creator of creation requires that there be some compatibility between the created order, including what can be determined by reason, and the order of faith. Therefore, it can be faithfully said that classical non-Christian and non-Jewish thinkers (for example, Plato, Aristotle, Seneca, Cicero) were able to perceive something of God's moral order for the common good. The political and civil order is for the common good of humanity and constitutes a sphere of God's rule, the conditions of which are perceivable by reason and distinct from, but in conformity with, revelation. Both partake in the one eternal law of God.

Thus the civil order (instituted by God)—that which is, so to speak, Caesar's (though more than mere government)—operates under the conditions of the created order of nature. As Aquinas says, "divine law, which comes from grace, does not destroy human law, which comes from nature."[9] Such is the law built into God's creation and inscribed upon our hearts, in which all people and societies can participate, and to which Christians have an obligation. Christian believers and well-meaning adherents of other faiths and persuasions have a basis for dialogue, and Christians in good conscience can participate in the public arena on the basis of universal human principles and the higher virtues of civil order, or as the statement "Evangelicals and Catholics Together" put it, in a manner that is "oriented to the common good and discussable on the basis of public reason."[10]

That there is a theological distinction requires that the two spheres of God's earthly order, that is, the civil (including governmental) and ecclesiastical, neither be institutionally merged, as medieval excesses tended toward, nor set against each other, as modern radical secularism, in effect, promotes. The Christian exists in both spheres and is called to accountability in both. At the same time the individual Christian as well as the church is especially called to further moral virtue and right order for society as a whole and to do so in a manner that does not violate the ordinances of God, either civil or ecclesiastical. Paraphrasing a classic formula, Christianity is an instrument of God's grace for the perfection of nature.

Christian Values and the Political Order

We live in a time of diminished political credibility, when we routinely ascribe base motives to our political leaders and the processes of government. We have come to expect political scandals, and our leaders continually oblige, scrounging for ethical lapses and indiscreet failings of their opponents, because discrediting someone's character wins political and legislative battles without having to win in the forum of ideas. Politicians and their media allies have fostered a political environment wherein scandal mongering and the criminalization of policy differences are the usual practice, where demonizing opponents rather than engaging their ideas has become the norm. And besides that, or perhaps because of that, most of us do not even bother to vote, much less take an active interest in civic affairs as free citizens ought. These degraded doings of politics are both a symptom of, and a contributor to, social disorder.

What values and attitudes ought Christians to bring to the public square? Without falling into naivete, life in the public square should be characterized by simple sincerity. In having to defend his credentials and the credibility of his message, Paul says: "We have renounced disgraceful, underhanded ways; we refuse to practice cunning or to tamper with God's word, but by the open statement of the truth we would commend ourselves to every man's conscience in the sight of God" (2 Corinthians 4:2). In a time when there were so "many peddlers of God's word" (2 Corinthians 2:17), Paul approached his mission in the public arena of his day with sincerity and in an aboveboard manner, depending on the truth and appealing to the conscience of his hearers. In the political sphere today we have an overabundance of those peddling ideologies, interests, and devious words at no small cost to the common good and the health of the commonwealth. Ideas should be presented in the public square and discussed and debated based on the merits of those ideas. Instead we often hear ad hominem harangues, demagogic rhetoric, and disingenuous twisting of opponents' ideas out of transparently partisan interest.

It has been noted that one of the hallmarks of Pauline thinking is the desire for peaceful and orderly relations, both within the Christian community and among outsiders. "For God has called us to peace," Paul says (1 Corinthians 7:15). Concord is a high quality and discordant qualities are to be avoided: "jealousy, quarreling, slander, gossip, conceit, and disorder" (2 Corinthians 12:20). We are to try to be congenial people and to live in peace (1 Corinthians 13:11). Such is not always possible in all situations, of course. In a debased political environment vigorous challenge must often be made, without, however, becoming ourselves that which we abhor. We are not called to be bystanders in the face of the perpetrators of chaos. Yet we know to what we should aspire and the negative qualities we should hope to put aside. Christians are a people who believe in the God who causes order out of chaos. The exorcisms of Jesus, puzzling to the modern mind, can at least be understood on a symbolic level as casting out the agents of chaos, which demons represent, to restore the original order and wholeness in creation and in people. Thus, Christianity should be a healing presence in the sociopolitical order.

Leaders are especially to exemplify the best of Christian qualities, particularly in regard to others. The second letter to Timothy says that the "Lord's servant must not be quarrelsome but kindly to everyone ... correcting his opponents with gentleness" (2 Timothy 2:24–25). Vociferous bombasts need not apply. Similarly, the good bishop is described as a person who, among other things, is above reproach, dignified, gentle, temperate, not quarrelsome, not conceited, and "well thought of by outsiders" (1 Timothy 3:2–7).

This concern to relate positively to all, to "command the respect of outsiders," is a characteristic of the Pauline approach (1 Thessalonians 4:12). Christians are to be people of moral virtue and not troublemakers, but it is also clear that you cannot hope to persuade, much less convert, those who have no respect for you. That should be a fundamental lesson for those in the public arena. That does not mean tepid engagement or tacit surrender, but Christians should represent the moral high ground. We should press and come to expect all leaders in the political arena to hold to higher standards of engagement. In discussing his handling of the Corinthians' contribution to the collection that he and his coworkers were raising, Paul says, "we aim at what is honorable not only in the Lord's sight but also in the sight of men" (2 Corinthians 8:21). That is a good motto for all involved in public life.

The Christian mission in this regard should be to restore a politics of elevation over degradation. The words of the *Federalist Papers,* number 57, are an effective application of the above Christian ideals to civil society: "The aim of every political constitution is or ought to be first to obtain for rulers, men who possess most wisdom to discern, and most virtue to pursue the common good of the society; and in the next place, to take most effectual precautions for keeping them virtuous, whilst they continue to hold their public trust."[11]

The good political order requires a proper conception of freedom. "For freedom Christ has set us free," Paul tells us. For we are "called to freedom" but it is a freedom to do what is right, not "freedom as an opportunity for the flesh" (Galatians 5:1, 13). The first letter of Peter tells us that we are to live as free people, yet without using our "freedom as a pretext for evil" (1 Peter 2:16). Our lexicon of freedom includes a sense of moral responsibility. The preface to the Decalogue, the heart of the faith tradition and moral code of the biblical people of God, places these fundamental religious and moral commandments in the context of God's liberating act: "I am the Lord your God, who brought you out of the land of Egypt, out of the house of bondage" (Exodus 20:2). God gives freedom and reveals how free people are to live. No social order can endure freedom without responsibility, and a society whose institutions of governance and culture celebrate freedom as only individual rights, freedom from the consideration of standards of propriety and moral principle, is a society at war with itself. Ours is a freedom that tries to give no offense, that tries to abide by legitimate custom, and that upholds the ideal of freedom rooted in moral order.

Surely one of the most fundamental philosophical causes of our social disorder is the separation of rights from their source in the Creator, who is truth and from whom comes moral order. The American founders understood this, exemplified in the Declaration of Independence: "We hold these truths to be self-evident, that all men are created equal, that they are endowed by their Creator with certain unalienable Rights." That is the language of the Enlightenment but it contains ideas in consonance with Christian faith—that something of truth is accessible by reason in creation; that all are equal, "neither Jew nor Greek," in the sight of God; that rights and freedom are derived from our created nature and our created nature presumes a moral order rooted in the Creator. The Declaration proclaims that government exists to "secure these rights." Government, therefore, serves the purpose of God, who is the author of these rights. People who are fundamentally free and recognize government as under God, or as the founders had it, "the Laws of Nature and of Nature's God," have the responsibility for "laying its foundation on such principles and organizing its powers in such form, as to them shall seem most likely to effect their Safety and Happiness." That is, government is "instituted by God" and is "God's servant for your good" and is "not a terror to good conduct, but to bad" (Romans 13:1, 3–4).

The form of government the founders finally designed, after the Articles of Confederation proved ineffective, was called federalism. "Federal" comes from a Latin word for "league." In essence the states formed a league with each other and established a central government with certain enumerated powers, chiefly in defense, foreign affairs, and interstate commerce.

A significant debate between the federalists and the anti-federalists was over the question of the promotion of virtue among the citizenry. Both sides recognized the necessity of a virtuous citizenry for any kind of republican government they would form. The anti-federalists feared the conditions for virtue would not be possible in a large republic. The federalists maintained that the practice of citizenship would mostly occur in the states and local communities since only certain limited functions applied to the central government.[12] Most questions of domestic policy would remain with the states.

Now that the federal government has far exceeded the bounds of its original limitations, it is precisely the question of virtue in society and good citizenship in our democratic republic that so occupies our concerns. If we want to restore the moral health of society, then part, but by no means all, of the answer is to empower the lower levels of government and encourage greater responsibility by individuals, families, and communities and the private sphere of society in general. That is, we must restore some semblance of our original federal system, returning to the states and people those powers that the federal government was not intended to have as envisioned by the Tenth Amendment. In this way we help to lay again the foundation for virtue and responsibility to flourish.

Federalism relates to a theological concept that originated in Catholic social teaching: subsidiarity. "Subsidiarity" is from a Latin word meaning "to help." Government is instituted to be a help, a servant for our good, as biblically affirmed. But more than that, it entails the proper ordering of the levels of sociopolitical organization so that needs are dealt with at the lowest possible level of effectiveness. Human dignity requires, and the Bible affirms, that what individuals can do for themselves, they ought to do. Likewise, the vigor of the family must not be weakened. No level of sociopolitical organization, such as the state, should by its policies tend to absorb the functions of individuals, families, and communities of association; and higher levels of sociopolitical organization should not absorb lower levels, lest the servant should become the master. Jesus said that our leaders are not to be like the kings of the earth who lord it over their subjects. Rather, "whoever would be great among you must be your servant, and whoever would be first among you must be your slave" (Matthew 20:25–27). And while that surely was addressed to the Christian community, we do well to apply that attitude to the public square as well. A democracy is a system of government in which the rulers are our servants.

Those who know Jesus as Lord know that the state cannot be made lord. The government that becomes all things, with all else subservient to its province, and comes to disregard its accountability to "the Laws of Nature and of Nature's God" has indeed pretended to make itself lord. Our political order has come to be more and more like the mob who handed Jesus over, saying, "we have no king but Caesar" (John 19:15). Since about the middle of this century, the federal government, especially through the judiciary, has gradually backed away from the public recognition of its accountability to the Creator; this even as government expanded greatly, absorbing many responsibilities of individuals and civil society and bringing under its bureaucratic control everything a dollar of government support touches. The "Evangelicals and Catholics Together" document well affirms the philosophical framework for the balance that should be restored:

> We strongly affirm the separation of church and state, and just as strongly protest the distortion of that principle to mean the separation of religion from public life. We are deeply concerned by the courts' narrowing of the protections provided by the "free exercise" provision of the First Amendment and by an obsession with "no establishment" that stifles the necessary role of religion in American life.[13]

The recognition of accountability to God through, among other ways, some form of public prayer in schools and other institutions of public life serves to reinforce that all, including the state, are morally accountable to Higher Authority and that there are limits to the pretenses of human government. It is not necessary to have daily classroom prayer to accomplish this, and indeed such accentuates the contentiousness over the question of the boundary between the sphere of the church and the sphere of the state and institutions of civil society. It is altogether appropriate, however, that public institutions, including schools, recognize their accountability to Higher Authority and the moral order through ceremonial public prayer when the institution as a whole is gathered or significantly represented, such as at graduations, assemblies, and sporting events. The hostility to religion masquerading as neutrality, so that moral discipline goes wanting, that textbooks present a distorted view of our country's religious heritage, that students cannot mention religious themes in their work, that religious students cannot gather as other extracurricular associations, that courtyards and school halls cannot display the religion-based cultural symbols of our holidays, ought to be overturned and the balance restored to America's civic order. The federal government makes itself god when it denies to the public square, down to the most local level, any symbolic representation of transcendent commitments.

The American founders' phrase, "Laws of Nature and of Nature's God," is reminiscent of Paul's discussion (referred to above) of pagan ability to know something of God and God's order through creation: "Ever since the creation of the world his invisible nature, namely, his eternal power and deity, has been clearly perceived in the things that have been made" (Romans 1:20); furthermore, "what the law requires is written on their hearts" (Romans 2:15). Government therefore is responsible to operate in accordance with God's rule through the created natural order and the moral constraints therein revealed. That the American founders saw government as so constituted is reinforced by the submission of their political action to the judgment of God: "appealing to the Supreme Judge of the world for the rectitude of our intentions" and relying on the "Protection of Divine Providence." Politics and civil society are accountable to God as evident through nature by moral reason, and the agencies of public life, including education, as well as the political-legal system, ought to recognize this as the most basic principle of civilization. We need to restore the American founders' respect for Providence and truth and, among other things, end our suicidal notion that anything government touches must forswear religious expression.

Conclusion

Christianity always related to the culture in which it lived, although it kept its ultimate and unique concerns in perspective. It built upon and sought to improve the best cultural values it found there and did not make itself a separatist, much less subversive, movement. Throughout history, for all the human faults in the church, Christianity has been a civilizing force and must now as much as ever step up to that challenge. God rules both through the "Laws of Nature" and through the work of the church. Government is instituted by God and operates in the natural sphere but must recognize its accountability to God and the moral order derived from God, in the manner of the American founding. Government is limited in scope and should not absorb the responsibilities of individuals, families, and communities, or those of the church, and it should be organized in such a way as to encourage virtuous citizenship.

Christians live both in the sphere of civil society, including the state, and in the church. They should, therefore, seek a harmonious relationship between the two without, however, merging the realm of the church and of the spiritual with the realm of Caesar and of civil society. The theistic language of the American founding and religious freedom, including a restored accommodation by government of appropriate religious expression, provide the basic philosophical framework for this. Along with this, the theological concept of the twofold rule of God, among other things, protects the authenticity and integrity of the church to be the church. The mission of the church is primarily spiritual in nature, and its involvement in the public square, as church, should focus first on proclaiming the gospel but also on upholding moral principles for civil society, without usually becoming entangled in politics and the machinations of mundane policy affairs, absent compelling justification. Politics is normally the forte of its members who are also citizens of the state. It is as good citizens, shaped by Christian values, that Christians should engage the political arena. We err if we think that ours is a mission to plant the kingdom of God on earth by means of government action. And we cannot expect to accomplish all things through the civil law. We must also, and fundamentally, persuade people to change their lives and attitudes.

Notes

1. Joseph A. Fitzmyer, *Romans,* vol. 33 of *The Anchor Bible* (New York: Doubleday, 1993), 141.
2. Ibid.
3. Richard J. Dillon, "Acts of the Apostles," in *The New Jerome Biblical Commentary,* ed. Raymond E. Brown, Joseph A. Fitzmyer, and Roland E. Murphy (Englewood Cliffs, N.J.: Prentice Hall, 1990), 754–55.
4. See Colossians 3:18–4:1; Ephesians 5:21–6:9; 1 Timothy 2:8–15, 6:2; Titus 2:1–10; cf. 1 Peter 2:18–3:7.
5. Thomas Aquinas, *Summa Theologica,* I-II, Q. 94, A. 2, in *The Political Ideas of St. Thomas Aquinas: Representative Selections,* ed. Dino Bigongiari, Hafner Library of Classics (New York: Hafner Publ. Co., 1953), 46.
6. See Ernest L. Fortin, "St. Augustine," in *History of Political Philosophy,* ed. Leo Strauss and Joseph Cropsey, 3rd ed. (Chicago and London: University of Chicago Press, 1987), 176–205.
7. For a current exposition of the twofold rule of God tradition, see Robert Benne, *The Paradoxical Vision: A Public Theology for the Twenty-first Century* (Minneapolis: Fortress Press, 1995).
8. See Dino Bigongiari, introduction to *The Political Ideas of St. Thomas Aquinas,* vii–xxxvii.
9. Thomas Aquinas, *Summa Theologica* II-II, Q. 10, A. 10, in *The Political Ideas of St. Thomas Aquinas,* xxxvii.
10. "Evangelicals and Catholics Together: The Christian Mission in the Third Millennium," *First Things,* no. 43 (May 1994): 20.
11. *The Federalist Papers by Alexander Hamilton, James Madison and John Jay,* with introduction and commentary by Gary Wills (Toronto and New York: Bantam Books, 1982), 289.
12. See Eugene W. Hickok, Jr., "Federalism, Citizenship, and Community," in *Building a Community of Citizens: Civil Society in the Twenty-first Century,* ed. Don E. Eberly (Lanham, Md.: University Press of America, 1994), 194–97.

13. "Evangelicals and Catholics Together: The Christian Mission in the Third Millennium," 19.

11

Culture Wars, Moral Wars

Michael Novak

We have just finished the bloodiest century in history. There is no guarantee that the next century will not be even bloodier. But we were engaged in this century in two great issues which I think are largely settled, at least on the level of ideas.

First, the proposition that dictatorship is better than democracy. Democracy is slow, even decadent, it was asserted. A dictator who is in touch with the people, who knows what to do, and does it, is better. That was the proposition held by many in this century. It was held until the dictators caused such vast bloodshed and abused human beings so horribly that today, while there are still lots of dictators around, only one or two of them still claim, or have the fortitude to claim, that dictatorship is better than democracy. The proposition has been soundly defeated in the *experience* of people. For all its faults, democracy is now seen as far better at protecting the rights of poor people, vulnerable people, individuals, and minorities.

The second great proposition put to the world, and one that too many worldly intellectuals believed, or tended to believe, is the following: Socialism is better for people than capitalism, especially for poor people, certainly morally better. It may not produce the goods, but it is morally superior. This proposition, too, is far less sustainable than it was only a decade ago. Most of the world, southern China, perhaps, most notably, is busy experimenting not only with private property and markets, which are important but not at the heart of the matter, but more importantly with enterprise. Most of the world is experimenting with allowing people to use their imagination, their own ideas about new products, new goods, and new services, in order to provide for their fellow human beings. That creative imagination is the heart of capitalism.

Those engaged in these experiments typically expect them in due course to lead to fuller respect for rights in the political sphere. Capitalism has been shown to be an empirical condition for democracy. There is no true democracy anywhere (respecting rights based on the rule of law, protecting minorities, ensuring checks and balances, and so forth) that does not have a capitalistic economy. When there are a sufficient number of successful entrepreneurs in China and a larger middle class, they will know that they are smarter than the generals and the commissars, and the demand for republican government will spread.

There were times in the twentieth century when the outcome was in question about resisting these two propositions. It was not at all certain that democracy and capitalism, the free society, in other words, would win. But what was seriously neglected in the twentieth century—even by the defenders of democracy and capitalism—was the moral, intellectual, and cultural sphere: the third foundation of a free society.

A free society has, then, three parts to it: a free polity, liberating us from torture and tyranny; a free economy, liberating us from poverty (most of us need to think back only two generations to come upon extreme poverty); and finally, the free moral or cultural system, the system which respects us as persons of conscience and inquiry, and judgment and intellect, who have great love for the arts and for beauty, and who allow the institutions in the moral-cultural sphere to be free. It is this third sphere which we have neglected.

The heart of culture is *cult*. It is peculiar to Judaism and to Christianity (and to Islam, which arises from the two of them) to have a cult in which the proper name of God is truth and being. A cult that the Benedictines were perhaps the key institution in spreading across Europe and thus making available to the whole world. The Benedictines are the *one* organization that took this cult and the key ideas associated with it and established them northwards all through Europe. They converted hunter peoples into civilized peoples and to peoples of the Book. They introduced Judaism and Christianity to peoples who knew nothing of it. It is no accident that Saint Benedict is the patron saint of Europe, or that the European medal has the image of Saint Benedict on it.

Benedictines were also, in a sense, the first multinational corporation, selling their wines and cheeses across national boundaries. And, indeed, the law of the corporation descends more from the laws of the Benedictines than from any other source; so does the notion that democracy should include everybody, not just the elite, but the youngest, and the poorest, even the most illiterate. The Benedictines were the first organization in which that sense of universality was true. We all owe a special debt to the Benedictines.

That said, three of our civilization's key ideas have fallen on a very hard, unfertile stretch of rock in the twentieth century: the ideas of truth, of liberty, and of the body. I am going to concentrate on the first, the idea of truth. But I will begin by briefly addressing the understanding of the human body and then the idea of liberty. More and more through all advanced societies, debates are moving into the moral-cultural sphere. If we're all going to be democracies, and we're all going to be capitalists in one form or another, we can argue around the margins of democracy and capitalism, and there's certainly a lot of detail to settle, but the really emotional issues, the really unsolved issues, are those in which what some people think of as good, other people think of as evil.

It is issues like that which are at the basis of the "culture wars." The culture wars are fought in moral wars. They tend to focus on our understanding of the human body. Just think of the debates which currently rack England, Sweden, France (France less so at the moment), Italy, Germany, and of course the United States. Increasingly they concern abortion and euthanasia.

If abortion means that for the first time in our history we allow to private citizens the right to inflict violence, without due process, on other human beings, this logic is going to come back to haunt us at the end of life. Homosexuality, sexuality, sex education—these are other issues that are now bombarding the political sector. The last place you should treat these things, however, is in the political sphere. Politics is not a set of institutions well designed to treat such subtle, universal, and all-embracing matters. But with the failure of all our other institutions, the unresolved issues are being thrust upon politicians.

In our value-free sociology, psychology, and other disciplines in the universities and in the language that flows from those disciplines into our literature, we have come to think of the human body in a very flat way. We think of it as unmysterious, uncomplicated, as simply a bundle of needs. You feel an urge, you feel a need, it demands to be satisfied, and there's no more moral judgment to be made.

Irving Kristol once commented that if a couple were to make love on a public stage in, say, Boston or New York, the only moral question some of his liberal friends would acknowledge is whether or not the "actors" were being paid the minimum wage.[1] Contrast that with the message of Corinthians: Do you not know that your body is the temple of the Holy Spirit? It's a very different way of imagining the human body.

Judaism was distinctive among the world religions of the Mediterranean basin in that at the very beginning of the Book it says that *man and woman*, he created them. This suggests that there is something extremely important in that difference. Moreover, it suggests that there is something extremely important in our understanding of God to be found in that difference. In some powerful, difficult-to-express way, the Creator, in making an image of himself, needed to make two. Two that belonged together, but still two. We don't know what God is. Nobody sees God. In Jewish terms, one should not even pronounce the name of God in order to respect his mystery. But whatever God is, he is more like the love, the friendship, between man and woman, the joining between man and woman, than he is like anything else.

We have here an extraordinarily vivid and powerful way of differentiating a whole culture of people from all other peoples. And with it came a certain set of moral codes: We owe our bodies, and one another, respect. But we are not allowed to talk this way in public today. If we don't talk this way in public today, how is the ethical code that comes with all this to be understood? We thus have a huge agenda to accomplish: to develop a theology and philosophy of the human body. We need to articulate what it means when we call the body sacred. We must begin to suggest what the dimensions are in which we understand a certain sacredness surrounding the body.

There is also the idea of liberty that we must address. We have at home two cats, a black-and-white cat and an orange cat. Our daughters brought home these cats when our daughters were very young, promising that we (my wife and I) would never have to take care of them. Our daughters have long since left home and we've still got the cats. My wife and I are leaving tomorrow for Rome, but we've got to find a "cat sitter." Can you believe it? You're sixty-two years old and you can't leave home until you find a cat sitter. Our cats are very different from one another. I hate cats, but I have to concede they have distinct personalities. Pepe LePeau is thin; Le Beau is fat. Pepe is so smart that it can't be believed. When he wants your attention, he'll move a plate or anything breakable, to the very edge of the dresser or table; then, he'll thump a little bit or catch your attention before moving the object just a little bit more. If you don't jump to get whatever he wants you to get, the object drops off. He knows you're going to get angry and hit him, you're going to swear at him. But after you've finished your tirade, you're going to try to figure out what it is he wanted.

Le Beau is not like that at all; Le Beau is very slow-witted. Yet one thing we do not have to worry about these cats is what career they are going to choose. Our cats do not *act*; they just *behave*. The way cats behaved in Egypt, I suppose, is the way cats behave today. They cannot but follow the law of their own nature. They do what they do by *instinct*. Our children are not like that: we can never predict what our children will do next. Our children act—and to act means to be able to form conceptions, images of a future different from any other, or to look on your past and repent of it, wishing you could have done things differently. It is the capacity to reflect and to choose. As far as we know, human beings are the only creatures in God's creation that are capable of doing this, with the implication being that we are free to follow or not to follow the law of our own nature. We do not act solely from instinct, which adds a whole dimension of tragedy and possibility to human life. In this way, we are like God; we know the difference between good and evil, alas. We are able to violate the law of our own nature knowingly. Of course, we have to come to know what the law of our own nature is—something we don't even know in the beginning. We have to discover it slowly, and some of us insist on discovering every bit of it for ourselves, the hard way, not learning from the wisdom of those who have tried and learned by mistake, by bloodshed, by suffering. We have to keep learning everything over and over and over. In any case, this is what makes human freedom the unique treasure that it is.

It is in this context that Tocqueville pointed out that in America, unlike in Revolutionary France, there was a distinction made between animal, or childish, liberty and human, or adult, liberty.[2] Childish liberty, like that of our cats, is liberty to do what you do by instinct. Whatever your instincts tell you to do, whatever you want to do, whatever you feel like doing, do it. With adult liberty, you do what you know you *ought* to do. It is the liberty to obey the law of your own nature with joy or reluctance.

In Dostoyevsky's *Brothers Karamazov*, Alyosha, learning from Father Zosima, said that saying yes is the heart of all prayer. Well, we have lost the difference between liberty as doing what you ought to do and liberty as doing whatever you want to do. Nobody is born free; freedom has to be earned. You have to learn the habits that allow you to reflect before you do things. This builds commitment so that other people can rely on your choices. That is what forms character.

When you are the sort of person whose choices can be relied upon by others, they quickly realize that they are dealing with someone of character. I loved overhearing our daughter say once to her friends, "Oh, I'll go in and ask them again, but when my mom says no, she means no." That's character: people can take your word, or more than your word—they can just take you as you portray yourself, and rely on you.

Of course, it is probably asking too much of human beings to expect to rely on them perfectly all the time. If men were angels, we could, but alas, men are not angels. That is why in the United States we say on our coins, "In God We Trust," the operational meaning of this being that we fully trust nobody else. We have checks and balances, the insight that makes our revolution different from the French Revolution. Human beings are capable of sin, so if you're going to create a free society, you cannot do it with utopian hopes; you need checks and balances. Because human beings are not capable of bearing total unchecked power, we need to recover the idea of liberty as self-rule. We need to teach it in our schools and in our daily life the way it used to be taught.

Self-government, self-discipline—Boy Scouts and Girl Scouts all know this; that's what they are all about. Once this idea permeated American society; we even recited poems about it in school. The nuns or the teachers in the public schools focused on how much character we showed and pointed out where our instincts and our restlessness were getting the better of us. You didn't learn poetry writing and penmanship by instinct, but through exercises, doing those *o*s over and over and over again, the big ones and the little ones, and so on.

Let us consider the idea of truth. It is a paradox of our age that the supporters of the Enlightenment no longer defend reason. First of all, people who call their movement "the Enlightenment" to distinguish themselves from the Benedictines and the Franciscans and all the others who stood for "the dark ages" are not exactly making a modest or humble claim. But they have been humbled in recent generations.

There are very few philosophers in the United States today who could say with Thomas Jefferson, even at the University of Virginia, "We hold these truths to be self-evident." Richard Rorty and others say contingency goes all the way down. In the conception of these thinkers, foundations do not exist. Looking for foundations, they say, is a mistake: There are no foundations for the American republic; there are no foundations for truth.

The other side of the paradox is that it turns out to be the religious people—the Jews, the Christians and perhaps, the Muslims—who have become the defenders of reason. They are born with an imperative to pursue the truth, and to pursue it wherever it leads.

Isn't it a marvelous paradox that those the Enlightenment despised turn out to be the defenders of reason when those who despised religion in the name of reason have abandoned reason? This is just an extraordinary turning of the world upside down, but that is indeed where we are. The name of the Creator that we Christians learn from Judaism is "he who is": being, reality, facticity. In a special sense, *that* is the being that lies behind all other facts; *that* is the fact that makes all the other facts true. And so we cannot possibly defend the God we love without defending truth and reason. Because how can Christianity begin to make truth claims when there is no longer respect for truth?

John Adams, our second president, once said that, in his opinion, the world owes more to the Hebrew people than to any other.[3] The Hebrew people, he said, made civilization possible. Adams does not explain exactly what he means by that claim, but I think he means this: No matter how wealthy or how powerful a people or a person becomes, they must always remember that they are going to face an undeceivable Judge. In other words, no matter how wealthy or how powerful you are, you can't buy the truth; it is just not for sale. There is always a truth much greater than you are which gives purchase to everyone else. Hence, Thomas Aquinas's definition: civilization is conversation. Civilized people persuade one another through argument because they respect each other's capacity for reason, in the light of truth, in the light of evidence. Barbarians, on the other hand, club one another. The notion that there is a truth and that we all stand under judgment by one who is undeceivable clears the ground for civilization. It gives all of us a focus of something beyond our own passions and prejudices and interests in whose light we are to be judged.

Something like this was recreated in the twentieth century in the darkest and most remote corners of the concentration camps, the jail cells, and the torture chambers.

If you read the concentration camp literature of the twentieth century, one thing will strike you. Even the atheists, absurdists, and nihilists (some of whom would have said that there is no truth; there is only contingency the whole way down) came to a point in their interrogations when it suddenly became very important not to sign their name to something that they did not believe. In other words, they reached a point where they knew they must not say "x" just because their jailers wanted them to say "x." If it was not true, they could not sign their name to it. Their jailers said to them (and you can read this in Arthur Koestler very vividly): "Don't kid yourself. You yourself have said there is no truth. Just sign here. You yourself have said everything is pragmatic. Just sign. We're going to be here for seventy years or one thousand years. This is the new order; get used to it. Nobody's going to know whether you signed or not." They found they could not do that; it did mean something. And, moreover, with hours and hours to think this over, they began to realize that there was within them a power or light which was greater than themselves. It was something over which they had no control and to which they felt they needed to be faithful. It did not take very long before most of them started calling this presence God. You can find evidence of this in the writings of Mihailo Mihailov, of Sakharov and Scharanski, and in the literature of the Second World War and the period afterwards. You can read about the rediscovery that truth matters, and that it matters because it is a relationship between our Creator and ourselves, or between the light in which we participate and ourselves. You know the light does not come from you alone because you can see your own distortions of it, your own weaknesses in it, your own betrayals of it; it is not you. You know you are being faithful to something that calls on you, and that makes demands on you.

Because this discovery was made at so much cost and under so much suffering in so many forgotten places, it is very important that we do not allow this lesson to be lost. To do so would give a posthumous victory to Hitler, Mussolini, Stalin, and the others, who, after all, began this great wave of bloodshed by arguing: There is no truth, there is no good, there is no evil. There is only opinion. Intellect has no purchase on reality, intellect cannot know moral truth, intellect cannot even know reality. What matters is will. What matters is preference. What matters is power. Those who accumulate power will decide what reality is. They will mobilize the whole population. They will overturn the foundations, turn the world upside down, and build a better world, build it the right way. But it is all based on the idea that there is only opinion.

I heard the graduate of a distinguished Catholic college say in his valedictory address just a few years ago: "One thing I learned at this institution over four years that I'm very grateful for is that everybody's values are as good as everybody else's." I wish I could report that his parents and his professors fainted on the spot, but I have a sneaking suspicion that they are also beginning to believe such things. But this is to give the victory to Hitler in the end. If there are only opinions—your opinion and my opinion and her opinion and his opinion and everybody else's opinion—then we are saying that intellect does not get to reality at all. If that is what is being said, then the way is opened to power. There will be nothing left to stand on in opposition to power. Facing the power, on what ground can you resist? This is why Vaclav Havel, president of the Czech Republic, is so insistent on the importance of truth. A sense of being, a sense of fidelity to truth, and of the power of a lie—it is hard to give these things names, but they are realities in life you can discover for yourself.

One of the arguments frequently used against those who appeal to the importance of truth is that it is simply a matter of fact that people do, across various cultures and within various cultures, disagree on important moral matters. It is not correct to conclude from that fact, however, that we should make relativism our moral principle. That there is great variety, many differences, and many arguments to be conducted, is certainly true. But to conclude from that observation that we cannot make discriminations among these alternatives in the light of evidence is not a solid inference.

We must insist that while no one of us can claim to hold the truth, the truth is greater than we are. We can all claim to want to submit to the truth and to follow the evidence where the argument leads us and where our tradition and sometimes our inarticulate convictions lead us. Often we cannot put into words everything that we know. We frequently do not quite agree with an argument, and on first hearing, if we can not come up with good answers for it, we will want to go back and reconsider our position. We will want to reach deeper into our tradition and come to understand what is at stake. Sometimes we know something is at stake, but what must be insisted on is that we judge these things in the light of the evidence.

Stephen Covey's book *Seven Habits of Highly Effective People* gives a vivid example of this. Covey describes the captain of an American battleship taking the bridge himself at night in the fog. Not long afterward, with the cold on his face, he spots through his glasses a light approaching almost directly ahead. He instantly orders his radio man to flash to the advancing ship, as he believes it is, to change course by so many degrees and in which direction. The signal is given, and the light flashes back; the radio man says, "Sir, he reports you should change course by so many degrees." To which the captain replies, "Well, you tell him I'm the rear admiral, the captain of this battleship, and he should change course." The flash comes back, "I am a seaman second class. This is the lighthouse."[4]

In the real world, the world as it is, there are rocks. In the real world, the mere existence of two different perceptions does not mean the perceptions are equivalent. Maybe they are; maybe they aren't. Let us look at the evidence. Respect for the reality principle is something we need to return to.

Finally, the notion of truth lies at the heart of what the ancients meant by virtue. There are four cardinal virtues, and they are of remarkable quality. They are all based on the notion of truth. One of them is *temperance*. Unless you have sufficient governance over your appetites and passions, you cannot see things straight at all. I have always argued that one of the most underexplained reasons for marriage is that it commits you for life to a person who is sworn to telling you all the things about yourself you don't want to hear. The first few times she does it, you might get angry and you don't believe what she is telling you. Sometimes it is only in the second or third telling that you begin to see the point. There are certain things about yourself you are so attached to, that it becomes difficult to believe that you could better yourself. In other words, we *do* get locked into certain habits and ways of doing things out of forms of self-love. We need to learn the virtue of temperance in order to overcome this.

Second, it often takes courage to see the truth. My wife will say things about me which I initially cannot deal with. I've got enough problems at the moment. But later on, the truth will sink in. It will only sink in when you have sufficient courage to take it on board, when you are not too tired with other things. Unless you have the courage to see especially painful things, you will not see them. So *courage* or *fortitude* is the second crucial habit.

The third virtue is *justice*. Giving to each moment, to each thing, to each person its due. Getting a sense of proportion, a sense of paying attention, a sense of noting the details. Most of us have a few people in different areas whom we like to consult when difficult decisions need to be made. I write out the reasons one way and the reasons the other way. Mondays, Wednesdays, and Fridays, I think I should do this; Tuesdays, Thursdays, and Saturdays, I think I should do that. Sundays, I pray. But there are some people I like to go to in order to discuss the matter in question with. It is astonishing how often they will pick out and highlight an aspect that I hadn't been paying enough attention to. That capacity to see what is important, to do justice to some aspect of reality, is a very important habit to acquire. People who have it are a great resource to have around.

These three virtues together give you the opportunity to acquire the fourth. It is called *prudence*, the virtue of practical wisdom (*phronesis* is the Greek word). It is the habit of seeing things truly and fairly. Aristotle described this and, finding he could not exactly define it, pointed to Pericles.[5] I can't define prudence because you have to be able to *see* what is important, what is vital in every single situation. There are not enough rules in the world to frame rules for this virtue. You have to form the habit of being a certain kind of person, and Aristotle points to the kind of person in question.

Reinhold Niebuhr, the great Protestant theologian, used to advise, in political matters, to look at the example of Winston Churchill.[6] Winston Churchill understood that decisions in the political and the ethical world are like decisions in a lifeboat. We do not always have a fixed position, nor can one always do it by the rules. But when the boat is lifting one way, you've got to lean very hard the other way. When it's lifting the other way, you have to go back. You must have a sense for the waters and the winds. The ability to make quick judgments, and true judgments, is a very important human characteristic. I have often been struck by the way in which my wife or other people I know do things like that. They just have an instinct, as good people often do. People who are good, who have a good will, who really want only the good, have a tendency to see things true and right.

These, then, are the four virtues: temperance, fortitude, justice, and prudence or practical wisdom. Our forebears thought these were the crucial virtues, the crucial habits that people must have if they want to see truly. We have to encourage one another in these all the time. Models of these virtues must be held up so that people learn what to do in different situations. It is a kind of learning that is quite situational because, as I have said, you can't get it out of a rule book. Human beings, heroes, living examples, are the best way to teach people. That is why we pay so much attention to saints in the Catholic Church. While none were perfect, they point us on the way.

I will conclude on this note. In the opening paragraph of the *Federalist Papers*, Alexander Hamilton writes that it was given to us for the first time in history to see whether or not a people might choose a form of government not by accident or power but through reflection and choice.[7] The authors of the *Federalist Papers* were making an appeal to their fellow citizens of New York to ratify the new Constitution of the United States since it would convey powers from the people to the government.

It was crucial that the argument be presented, and that the argument get past the prejudices and passions and ambitions and interests of the people of New York. Hamilton thus appealed to the virtue of the people of New York. We know, he reasoned, that you will be able to set aside your passions and your bigotries and your interests and attend to the argument because it is a matter so weighty, involving the destiny not only of our state but of our whole people and of the whole republican experiment. In fact, perhaps the fate of mankind hinges on the decision you make. That appeal, I want to emphasize, runs through our entire history as a nation. Americans were conspicuous for their capacity to do these four humble things: to be temperate; to be brave; to be just, giving to everything its due proportion; and to be prudent, to be wise in matters of practice.

It is a shame to live in a country whose ideas in the political and economic sphere have triumphed just at a moment when we are being so unfaithful to our cultural inheritance. The only way we can reverse direction is by starting over with the basic ideas, and recovering the appropriate habits that go with them. The terrible thing about moral reform is that you cannot start with other people, although such a course of action would often be easier. We have to start instead with ourselves and we have to start with small groups. It is not something government can do, but it is something that associations of free women and free men have to do.

I think that we are at the beginning of a great awakening. Throughout the country men and women are worried that we are not as good a people as our grandparents in certain respects were, although in some ways we have made advances beyond them. But in terms of character, I think people fear we are not as good. We cannot rely on one another as we used to be able to rely on one another. As a consequence, I think there is only a chance for reform, since there is nothing determined about our fate. We are made in the image of God in the sense that we are provident of our destiny, that we have a responsibility to make that destiny, and that there is nothing condemning us in advance. But we do have a great deal of work to do. We need to begin in many small communities and hope that the prairie fire lights up in one small community after another.

Notes

1. Irving Kristol, "On Conservatism and Capitalism," Wall Street Journal, September 11, 1975, in *The Neoconservative Imagination: Essays in Honor of Irving Kristol*, ed. Christopher DeMuth and William Kristol (Washington, D.C.: AEI Press, 1995), 187.

2. See Alexis de Tocqueville, *Democracy in America*, ed. J. P. Mayer, trans. by G. Lawrence (New York: Anchor Books, 1966), 46.

3. See the letter from John Adams to F. A. Vanderkemp, February 16, 1809 in The Works of John Adams, ed. C. F. Adams, vol. 9 (Boston: Little Brown, 1854), 609–10.

4. Stephen Covey, *The Seven Habits of Highly Effective People* (New York: Simon and Schuster, 1989), 33.

5. Aristotle, *Nichomachean Ethics* (Cambridge, MA: Harvard University Press, 1926), bk. 6, chap. 5, sec. 1140b, ll. 8–11.

6. Reinhold Niebuhr, "Winston Churchill and Great Britain," in *Christianity and Crisis*, vol. 15 (May 2, 1955), 51–2.

7. Alexander Hamilton, James Madison, and John Jay, *The Federalist Papers*, int. by C. Rossiter (New York: NAL 1961).

Index

abortion, 25–26, 89n18, 115;
Supreme Court on, 78, 82–83,
87
abuse in families, 15, 20, 42
Adams, John, 58, 118
adolescents: as criminals, 17, 20;
teen pregnancies, 13, 19. *See
also* children
AFDC. *See* welfare policies
affirmative action programs, 38,
42, 45, 47, 70
African Americans. *See* blacks
Alien Nation (Brimelow), 34
Anderson, Sherwood, *Winesburg,
Ohio*, 6
Annie Casey Foundation, 18
Aquinas, Saint Thomas. *See*
Thomas Aquinas, Saint
Aristotle, 47n2, 101, 121
Articles of Confederation (U.S.),
107
Asians, 34, 38
Augustine, Saint, *The City of God*,
103

Babbitt (Lewis), 6
*Basic Writings on Politics and
Philosophy* (Marx and Engels),
64n1
behavior. *See* virtues
Ben Casey (television show), 53,

56nn1–2
Benedictines, 114, 117
Benedict, Saint, 114
Bennett, William, *The Book of
Virtues*, 75
Besharov, Douglas J., 58
Blackmun, Harry A. (U.S. Supreme
Court Justice), 78, 82–83
blacks, 32n1, 70; and rates of father
absence, 16–17; values and
virtuous behavior in, 29–32
Blankenhorn, David, *Fatherless
America*, 16
block grants, 46, 47
Book of Virtues, The (Bennett), 75
Brimelow, Peter, *Alien Nation*, 34
Broder, David, 20
Bronfenbrenner, Urie, 17
Brothers Karamazov
(Dostoyevsky), 117
Burke, Edmund, 3

Cambodians, 39
capitalism, 113–14
Casey, Planned Parenthood v., 78
Catholic Church, 72, 81, 122;
governing capabilities of,
87–88; on political morality,
84–85
Catholic Encyclopedia: "Catholic
Social Doctrine" (Royal), 47n2;

64n1

mass media. *See* popular culture;
television
Masters of the Dream (Keyes), 29
Mead, Margaret, 22
media. *See* popular culture;
television
Memoir on Pauperism
(Tocqueville), 60–61
mental illness, 6–7
Miller, John, 21
Mill, John Stuart, 72; *On Liberty*,
3, 4; *The Spirit of the Ages*, 3–4
minorities. *See* ethnic and racial
minorities; immigration
Minow, Newton, 50
modernism, 4
morality, 2, 45, 84–85; and
demoralization of society,
67–70; language of, 74–75;
legislation of, 73–74; and
remoralization of society,
70–75. *See also* Christian
principles in public life
Mormonism, 87–88
motherhood, 18–19. *See also*
family; women
Moynihan, Daniel Patrick, 19–20,
70
MTV, 56
multiculturalism, 39–40, 70. *See*
also immigration
Muslims, 87–88, 117

National Endowment for the Arts
(U.S.), 70
natural law, 43, 44–45
Neibuhr, Reinhold, 121
Newsweek magazine, 75
New York Times, 56
Nietzsche, Friedrich Wilhelm, 72
Nude Descending a Staircase
(Duchamp painting), 4

NYPD Blue (television show), 56n2

On Liberty (Mill), 3, 4
On Religion (Schleiermacher), 80
order, ix; civil order and reason,
102–4; political order and
values, 104–9
Out of the Barrio (Chavez), 35
out-of-wedlock births. *See*
illegitimacy

Patterson, Orando, "Backlash,"
32n1
Pericles, 121
Philo (early Jewish thinker), 100
Pius XI, *Quadragesima Anno*, 47n2
Planned Parenthood v. Casey, 78
Plato, *Charmides*, 64
pluralism, ix–x, 15, 39–40
Political Liberalism (Rawls),
83–84, 89n8
politics, 115; core principles as part
of, 41–43, 46–47; traditional vs.
secular views of, 44–45. *See*
also government
popular culture, 49–50. *See also*
television
pornography, 55, 62, 65n8, 70
Portugal, 60
postmodern era: future of cities in,
61–62; ideology of, ix–x, 1, 66;
religion in, 81–82, 86
poverty, 13, 17–19, 60–61. *See*
also welfare policies
prayer, public, 87n18, 108;
Supreme Court on, 77–79
Proposition 187 (Calif.), 33–34, 38
prosperity, benefits and dangers
of, 57–61
Protestantism, 72, 81, 87–88
Protestant Reformation, 72
prudence, 100, 120–21
psychotherapy, 42–43, 44

About the Contributors

T. William Boxx is chairman of the Philip M. McKenna Foundation in Latrobe, Pennsylvania. He is the chief executive officer of the foundation, which concentrates on public policy and educational affairs. He also serves as a fellow in culture and policy with the Center for Economic and Policy Education at Saint Vincent College in Latrobe, Pennsylvania. He is the chairman of the board of the Commonwealth Foundation for Public Policy Alternatives and is on the boards of the Intercollegiate Studies Institute and the Henry Salvatori Center at Claremont McKenna College. He and Gary M. Quinlivan are coeditors of *The Cultural Context of Economics and Politics* (University Press of America, 1994), *Public Policy and the Restoration of a Civil Society* (Center for Economic and Policy Education, 1995), and *Policy Reform and Moral Grounding* (Center for Economic and Policy Education, 1995). He also contributed a chapter entitled "Building the Well-Ordered Society: Subsidiarity and Mediating Structures" to *Building a Community of Citizens: Civil Society in the Twenty-first Century*, edited by Don Eberly. Boxx received an M.A. in theology, summa cum laude, from Saint Vincent Seminary in 1992 and is a Ph.D. candidate in theology at Duquesne University. A native of Arkansas, he received his B.A. in sociology from Arkansas State University.

Linda Chavez is the president of the Center for Equal Opportunity. She is the author of *Out of the Barrio: Toward a New Politics of Hispanic Assimilation.* She is a syndicated columnist who has a weekly column with *USA Today.* Chavez writes often for many other publications including the *Wall Street Journal*, the *Washington Post*, the *New Republic, Commentary,* and *Crisis.* She makes regular appearances on PBS's *To the Contrary*, CNN's *CNN and Co.*, and CNBC's *Equal Time* and as a political commentator on *The McNeil-Lehrer News Hour.* She also serves as U.S. expert on the United Nations Subcommission on Human Rights. Chavez has held a number of political positions, among them White House director of public liaison (1983-85) and director of the U.S. Commission on Civil Rights (1983-85).

136 Culture in Crisis and the Renewal of Civil Life

Midge Decter is a distinguished fellow of the Institute on Religion and Public Life. She has written three books: *The Liberated Woman and Other Americans*; *The New Chastity*; and *Liberal Parents, Radical Children*. Her work, primarily in the field of social criticism, has appeared in a number of periodicals including *Harpers*, the *Atlantic*, and the *New Republic*. Decter is a regular and frequent contributor to *Commentary*. She is a member of the boards of the Heritage Foundation, the Center for Security Policy, and Resistance International and a member of the Council on Foreign Relations. For ten years, she was the executive director of the Committee for the Free World. She appears frequently on radio and television and lectures widely on a range of subjects from the family to American foreign policy.

Don E. Eberly is a founder and president of the Commonwealth Foundation, a nonpartisan public policy "think tank." He is also a founder and president of the National Fatherhood Initiative. He spent eight years in Washington in various key positions in Congress, the White House, and for presidential candidate Jack Kemp. Eberly is the author of *Restoring the Good Society: A New Vision for Culture and Politics*. He is the editor of *The Content of America's Character: Recovering Civic Virtue; Building a Community of Citizens: Civil Society in the Twenty-first Century;* and *Leading Pennsylvania into the Twenty-first Century: Policy Strategies for the Future*. He has written on numerous civil society and public policy subjects. Eberly received M.A.s from both George Washington University and Harvard University and has done doctoral studies at Pennsylvania State University.

Heather R. Higgins is the executive director of the Council on Culture and Community. She is also a senior fellow at the Progress and Freedom Foundation. She has been an editorial writer for the *Wall Street Journal* and an assistant editor at the *Public Interest*. Higgins is a frequent political commentator, appearing on such shows as CNN's *CNN and Co.*, PBS's *To the Contrary*, and Comedy Central's *Politically Incorrect*. She cohosts, with Newt Gingrich, *The Progress Report* on NET. Higgins is first vice president of the Women's National Republican Club. She also serves as a board member of the W. H. Brady Foundation and the Hoover Institution and as an advisory board member of the Donner Foundation's New Leadership Fellows Project. Higgins received her M.B.A. in finance from New York University.

Gertrude Himmelfarb is professor emerita of history at the Graduate School of the City University of New York. Himmelfarb received her doctorate from the University of Chicago in 1950. She has been the recipient of many honorary degrees and has received fellowships from the Rockefeller Foundation, the Guggenheim Foundation, the National Endowment for the Humanities, the Woodrow Wilson Center, the American Council of Learned Societies, the American Philosophical Society, and the American Association of University

Women. She is a fellow of the British Academy, the Royal Historical Society, the American Philosophical Society, the American Academy of Arts and Sciences, and the Society of American Historians. In addition to having served on the editorial board of the *American Historical Review*, the *American Scholar*, and other journals, she is on the Board of Trustees of the Woodrow Wilson International Center, the Council of Scholars of the Library of Congress, the Council of Academic Advisors of the American Enterprise Institute, and the Board of Advisers of the Library of America; until recently, she was on the Council of the National Endowment for the Humanities. She has written extensively on Victorian England. Her latest book is *The De-Moralization of Society: From Victorian Virtues to Modern Values.*

Russell Hittinger is the Warren Professor of Catholic Studies with the Department of Philosophy and Religion at the University of Tulsa. He is also a research fellow at the American Enterprise Institute for Public Policy Research in Washington, D.C. Hittinger authored the book *A Critique of the New Natural Law Theory* and edited two other books. His articles have appeared in *Review of Metaphysics*, *Review of Politics*, and *International Philosophical Quarterly*, as well as several law journals. He has been a visiting professor at Princeton University and at New York University. He was associate professor in the School of Philosophy at Catholic University of America. In 1991, he received the Silver Gavel Award of the American Bar Association for his article "Privacy and Liberal Legal Culture." Hittinger is a member of the editorial boards of the *American Journal of Jurisprudence* and *First Things: A Monthly Journal of Religion and Public Life*, and of the Fordham University Press Series in Moral Philosophy and Theology. He received his Ph.D. in philosophy from St. Louis University.

Glenn C. Loury is a professor of economics at Boston University and the Chairman of the Center for New Black Leadership. He previously taught economics and public policy at Harvard, Northwestern, and the University of Michigan. Loury has published many scholarly articles in the fields of microeconomic theory, industrial organization, natural resource economics, and the economics of income distributions. In addition to his work as an economic theorist, he has been actively involved in public debate and analysis of the problems of racial inequality and social policy toward the poor in the United States. His essays and commentaries have been featured in the the *New York Times*, the *Wall Street Journal*, the *Public Interest, Commentary*, the *New Republic,* and many other publications. Loury has been a visiting scholar at Oxford University, Tel Aviv University, the University of Stockholm, and the Institute for Advanced Study in Princeton. Loury is the recipient of a Guggenheim fellowship. He received his Ph.D. in economics from the Massachusetts Institute of Technology.

Culture in Crisis and the Renewal of Civil Life

Michael Novak, former U.S. ambassador, is the George Frederick Jewett Chair in Religion and Public Policy at the American Enterprise Institute in Washington, D.C., where he also serves as director of social and political studies. He has written some twenty-five influential books in the philosophy and theology of culture, including *The Catholic Ethic and the Spirit of Capitalism* and *This Hemisphere of Liberty*. He is the author of numerous monographs and over two hundred articles and reviews. He is copublisher of the monthly journal *Crisis*. Novak has received numerous awards including the Templeton Prize for Progress in Religion (1994); the Anthony Fisher Prize (1992); the Ellis Island Medal of Honor (1986); the position of first U.S. member, Argentine National Academy of Sciences, Morals, and Politics (1985); and twelve honorary degrees both in the United States and abroad. Novak serves on the editorial boards of several publications in the United States and abroad. He was cofounder of *This World, Crisis,* and *First Things*. He received his M.A. in history and philosophy of religion from Harvard University.

Gary M. Quinlivan is the executive director of the Center for Economic and Policy Education. He is chairman and a professor of the economics department at Saint Vincent College. He is the director of the center's Alex G. McKenna Series, the Clergy-Business Dialogue, and the Government and Political Education Series. He is a research fellow and member of the advisory board of the Allegheny Institute. Quinlivan is also the editor of the center's publications: *Economic Directions* and *Policy Visions*. Quinlivan has several publications on international trade and finance, authored several op-ed pieces, and coedited three books with T. William Boxx. From 1988 to 1989, Quinlivan was a Fulbright Scholar at Shandong University in People's Republic of China. In 1993, he received the Saint Vincent College Professor of the Year award. Since 1989, he has been an adjunct faculty member at Carnegie-Mellon University (economics department). Quinlivan is on the board of directors of the Westmoreland Economic Education Foundation. Quinlivan has a B.A. from the State University of New York at Geneseo and a Ph.D. in economics from the State University of New York at Albany.

Robert Royal is the John M. Olin Fellow in Religion and Society and vice president at the Ethics and Public Policy Center in Washington, D.C. He has written or edited eleven books, including *1492 and All That: Political Manipulations of History*; *A Century of Catholic Social Thought*; and *Play, Literature, Religion: Essays on Intercultural Textuality*. Royal has written numerous articles and reviews and has given speeches at colleges and universities throughout North America. He is also a review panelist for the National Endowment for the Humanities and is founder of the Washington *Cercle des Études Tomistes*. Royal has been honored with the Renaissance Society of America Summer Fellowship (Florence, Italy), a Fulbright Fellowship (Florence, Italy), and Who's Who among Rising Young Americans. Royal received his Ph.D. in comparative literature from Catholic University of America.

James Q. Wilson is the James Collins Professor of Management at the University of California in Los Angeles. He was previously the Henry Lee Shattuck Professor of Government at Harvard University. He is the author or coauthor of thirteen books, including *The Moral Sense, Thinking about Crime,* and *Varieties of Police Behavior.* Wilson has served on a number of national commissions concerned with public policy. He was chairman of the White House Task Force on Crime in 1966, chairman of the National Advisory Commission on Drug Abuse Prevention in 1972–73, a member of the Attorney General's Task Force on Violent Crime in 1981, and a member of the President's Foreign Intelligence Advisory Board from 1985 to 1991. Until 1993 he was chairman of the Board of Directors of the Police Foundation. He is currently chairman of the Board of Academic Advisors of the American Enterprise Institute, a trustee of the RAND corporation, and a director of the New England Electric System. He has honorary degrees from six universities. He received his Ph.D. from the University of Chicago.